I0050770

WEALTH INNOVATIVE

THE NEWEST & MOST INNOVATIVE
FORM OF BUSINESS OWNERSHIP

BY

JOSH BIEBER

CONTENT

Preface

The notion of writing this guidebook was an exciting proposition. I'm not motivated by attention or being in any potential spotlight. Instead, I wanted to just write something that could help others. Most of all, I sense the frustration many people are feeling, especially now, because of the increasingly difficult environment we live in. We are afforded so many more options and avenues today, but it actually just adds more and more dirt to the tunnel we have to dig to find the good opportunity.

Being able to help others is really what came to mind first. Initially, I was just sharing my experience with very few friends or colleagues who I thought could benefit. The model is so universal that literally anyone can simply plug-n-play.

Perhaps like you, I never planned on making a living in real estate, let alone the building industry. My father migrated to this country in 1955. In hindsight, I earned some of my personality from him. There was my father, with no education, coming to the US for a better life. With my mother, he made a decent living as well. He has money in the stock market, even more tucked away, a 2nd home in Florida; I'd call that a success. On the other hand, you have millions of college students, or recent grads, who don't know up from down. I was one of them.

I had my share of good times in college, but the last two years at University of Wisconsin is really when I got my act together. If I was to be accepted to grad school or attend a PhD program, I' had to get my grades up. So, that is exactly what I did. Overnight I gave up the bar scene for the library. Raising my GPA from a 2.3 to a 3.86 gave me a shot. I went from talking shop with the bartender to expanding my mind with professors.

After graduating I picked up an entry level position with a medical research program or two. They were all small resume builders intended to boost my grad school application. It was a casual conversation with a college friend, Joshua W., who I hadn't seen in quite a while, where I was exposed to the world of mortgage brokering and banking. This was a man with the grades and background of a Medical School student, but decided otherwise. Joshua was driving two cars, owned his own home and had a pair of jet-skis to boot. On the other hand, I was humping a bicycle everyday to a low paying job that barely covered the inflated rent!

After giving me the low down of what he did, I instantly dropped my grad school plans and went in a different direction. I don't recall what it was that attracted me to it so intensely. It was likely not the mortgage business just in itself, but rather the opportunity of being independent, being in control of my own income, my own destiny. Sure, he was doing well, but he was also working for himself. I'll take the chance of falling on my face any day if it means calling my own shots.

Many people are afraid of independence and love the warm blanket of a predictable paycheck, 30 minutes to scarf down lunch, and being confined to a cubicle for 40 hours a week just to get the rare belly rub from their boss. A predictable paycheck is what I had at the time and it made me stir-crazy. To know that in 4 months, or 4 years that I'll be paid approximately the same thing was something I couldn't come to grips with. Having corporate meetings highlighting the extra 4% I could make if I only turn myself over to the company resembled a defendant taking a plea-bargain.

To tell you the truth, I've been fired from more than one job in my life. In fact, I was 'terminated' from my research Project Coordinator position before jumping head first into the mortgage business. All the nurses and Doctors would prep the staff for a new incoming study with a simple 1-2 page printout of what the study entailed, its intentions, and how/what tests and procedures would be performed. It was the same simple procedure before, while and after I was there.

When testing a new pharmaceutical drug, the study is run like a boot camp. Blood draws and other examinations must be performed on the exact minute, even second. It was so time-sensitive that each volunteer would have to be observed taking their first bite of breakfast, lunch, and dinner at a specific predetermined time. We'd give a volunteer their food and count down from 10 to 0, which is when the meal would begin. Trust me when I tell you that these studies take nothing for granted. You can have a bad hair day and the Doctors will want to know why.

Before being fired from this illustrious career, I came up with my own PowerPoint presentation putting on a one-man show. I just saw the opportunity and thought it was a cleaner and more efficient seminar than what they were doing up until that point. Everyone stressed how darn perfect every study needed to be, but then reviewed the details in a less than state of the art approach. It took 10 more hours to generate the PowerPoint rather than the 1 hour I could have spent just hand writing it on paper like everyone else did. However, still, all they saw was this young fellow with apparently no respect for how they did things. Mind you, it appeared to me that 'how they did things' was the same for 20 years. Forget about the fact that how they were doing things could be improved. That wasn't important, evidently. I must have been this crazy wild man for actually incorporating 20th century technology into their Flintstones way of doing things.

Everything I did was with a precocious, innocent-minded intention. I don't complicate things. If it could be better, then change it. If you find out that the original way of doing things is actually better, then go back to that format. I'm not here for points or to win a popularity contest. Successful people can care less about the impression they might make. Impression is based on a public or collective perception. And people are indecisive and obtuse as a whole. People don't make progress because they are all looking at each other waiting for a sign. A person with an idea makes progress because he is not concerned or distracted by other people.

I jumped head first into the mortgage business working as a broker. The major issue was the mere fact that the office was 2 hours away. Thus, I was working as a loan officer out of my apartment. With no skills or training, I just went out and acted like I knew what the heck I was talking about. I picked up on the very basic math of a mortgage loan and just sold it. I was familiar with the basic brick. However, building a brick wall was the last thing I could do. Despite naivety, I developed some contacts.

I met Tricia R., a top 3 selling realtor in the county. Trish appreciated my attitude and personality. I didn't throw all the mortgage jargon or what we could necessarily do that other banks couldn't. I just shot the proverbial BS. She was being recruited by the manager at Countrywide Bank, however, Trish insisted she was already tied to a banker, me. She went on to explain that I just wasn't happy. Of course, any loan officer that was tied to this realtor was a catch for the manager. Needless to say, two weeks later I was working for Countrywide Bank.

I still really had no idea what I was doing but acted as if I did. However, it was time to drop the veil and really learn the business. After a few months, I had it down. Things were going pretty well, but a lot of my business was coming from New York City.

My father is a respected man in our Brooklyn, NY neighborhood. With his numerous contacts that he's earned over his time, closing loans in NY made a lot of sense.

We live in a different world nowadays. I believe that the more options you have, the harder it is. Moreover, the world is so connected and commercialized which just adds to the pressure. Every day we are surrounded by Facebook, Celebrity Award Shows, quick-buck schemes or another idiot who wants to present his prospectus on some apparently new energy drink. It's so difficult to find the straight line in all of it because we are barraged with information.

In more ways than one, ignorance is bliss. My father came to this country and thought 'I need to make money'. So he went out and did just that. After getting off the boat, he wasn't handed a list of 175 majors he could pick up from Brooklyn College. Getting a college degree wasn't enforced as a necessity. My father turned on the TV and 2500 channels didn't come up either. It was a simpler world. He left the house in the morning and made what he could with the resources around him. I believe the exact same thing applies today. Get out and use the resources around you and you'll likely be more successful than scouring the internet or calling 800 numbers off TV Private Programming shows. Therefore, the more options, the harder it is to find the real deal. We really over complicate things today.

Just the other day an anchor on a major cable network reported a story about how vegetables can actually be risky. Thirty seconds later she informed use that we're in a Depression and all the banks are folding. Not only were my vegetables unhealthy, but everything was burning down. I ran out of my house screaming into the middle of the street because I thought we were under attack! TV represents a type of publicly organized message that is assumed to be universally accepted. Everything, including the commercials, is so professionally staged, they must be true, right? In reality, we are so ill-informed it's not funny anymore. Just like a sit-com, every news channel has advertisers to answer to.

In addition to my fathers help, I also put together some referral sources on my own time. However, instead of having to lock loans through a 3rd party, I would transfer to a NY branch. Some banks are individually state licensed, which means your have to temporarily hand the ball off to a branch that is licensed in the target state to lock the loan. After which, you re-gain control of the deal and move on. Either way, I couldn't stand having to fumble around with another person, play phone tag, etc. The whole operation was inefficient. I therefore decided to transfer to a NY branch.

My colleagues thought I was out of my mind. First of all, they were all from Wisconsin, so leaving was impossible. They didn't have a network of referral sources from anywhere else. Maybe it's just me, however, I told you that if something could be done better, I just went for it. I didn't intend to hurt my manager's feelings. Sorry, it's best for me; it makes sense, see you later!

Things were going well for some time. I was making some nice money in the market. After all, NY loans are quite bigger and there are certainly more of them! However, the music stopped, the lights turned on and the party was over, literally overnight. All of a sudden, your friends were almost your enemies. The processors and underwriters who were closing loans were all of a sudden strangers. Not like they were doing personal favors before, but now, they couldn't get anything done. It was a nightmare. My income stopped dead in its tracks.

I followed my manager, who had left for Indymac. It was maybe 2 months into my shiny new employment when I received a funny email in my inbox. It stated that my position was being eliminated in 30 days. I had just gotten to this new bank, took the time to learn the ropes and meet the staff, and then I get this email! I called my manager and carefully mentioned something along the lines of 'I got this weird email. I don't know what I did, but it says my position is being terminated'. His response was 'Yep, about 4,200 of us got that email'. I was exhausted. Everything was out of my control. I went from one place to another at the complete mercy of the company, the managers, etc. I was getting tossed around like an animal in a tornado.

I've dabbled in some very large commercial real estate transactions. They are exciting and extraordinarily unique. Unlike residential real estate, the commercial world is incredibly slow moving and often times never lead to a close. Both the $320 million building in Manhattan and the $2.5 billion resort on the Las Vegas strip were two deals in a constant tailspin. The potential pay off always kept me in the game. We were close at times, but none of them ever panned out. Most never amount to anything.

The residential world is as reliable as it gets. Despite the market, you won't have prices dropping 50%. Commercial real estate is much more violent because it more closely resembles an investment. You've seen stocks tumble thousands of percent. Commercial real estate is not the same, but it is farther from the reliability of the residential market. After all, everybody needs a home. Not everybody is exactly in the market for a 65-story building.

Residential real estate is protected by RESPA (Real Estate Settlement Procedures Act), Truth in Lending and other government or bank guidelines. If the money is anywhere associated with Fannie Mac or Freddie Mac, you can bet it will be clean as a whistle. Borrowers cannot be charged more than a maximum percent on a loan and everybody has equal opportunity to buy a home. If a commercial real estate deal required your first born, Social Services won't be coming around to protect you!

My Builder

There was a particular builder in Madison who I always wanted to work with. It was still during the time when I was under the Madison, WI Countrywide branch. Mind you, I never left Madison when I was working for the NY Branch. It was simply a few changes in the system and the stroke of a pen. We live in a connected, highly technological world. I didn't have to sit in an office in NY to work there. Just like the people on the other end of the 800-number locking loans for you. I could never understand why you'd want to dial an 800 number to close a loan. It would make some sense for a home equity line of credit, but not an important loan such as a purchase. You want some personal customer service, especially if you are meeting a deadline.

In any event, this builder was producing gorgeous homes all around the city. The guy was a genius who did nothing but work hard and earn his keep. What caught my eye were the many different styles. You'll have some builders who can build your traditional bi-level home. Some subdivisions are just filled with the same fashioned home, just maybe in different colors. What's the point? It looks monotonous. Later in this guidebook, I talk about remodeling which addresses this issue of breaking the monotony of a home.

The builder, Dave, and I never got to meet, work together, etc. He wouldn't return a phone call or email, but I never took it personally. First of all, I was just another loan officer. Most importantly, why would you break up a good thing going? He had his one or two bankers that got him all the friggin' money in the world and delivered it immediately. The bank relationships were in stone and that's all there was to it. I was pretty convinced that I'd never get to work with him. I already accepted that fact once I transferred to the NY branch.

You can't walk into Walgreens and tell the manager you have a whole new pharmacy program they should use. It would involve changing the orientation of the shelves and getting new computers. Are you kidding me? Money is flooding in so fast that they can't stay ahead. No way would they change a thing and you can't blame them! Would you?

But not so fast; the market took a torpedo. This is when everything changed, and I mean everything. I was let go from Indymac, where I picked up a position at a correspondence bank. A bank with correspondence is one who closes the loan with their own limited money, but immediately sells the paper to a major bank like a Chase or a Wells Fargo. A mortgage broker is one that never actually funds the loan. They don't have a dime. They simply connect or 'broker' a bank to their client, acting as an intermediary. The disadvantage is the red tape of the entire wholesale sector which a broker must use. The rules and requirements are tremendously strict. The wholesale bank will underwrite a loan with a fine tooth comb and can drive you nuts. However, it is worth it for the broker because the potential profit is enormous. Nevertheless, I was working for a correspondent bank, which was not exactly a life in heaven. Things were moving slowly. It was like a bad game show.

Dave was going through his own problems, which I wasn't aware of because I never met the guy. Although, one day, I get the call and it's Dave on the other end of the phone. His lack of enthusiasm just sounded like he talked to 150 people before he finally called me. Dave began to explain that he has a great deal, but just can't push it through. Remember those bankers who were servicing every request of his? That untouchable Walgreens program I analogized? Well, it all broke down! None of it was working anymore. The music was over. Dave used to be able to pick up his cell phone, call a number, and have $1 million waiting. It was as easy as ordering a pizza. Now, he couldn't get $10 in change extended to him!

The opportunity knocked, I got the call, and I gobbled it up. I waited 3 years to talk to this guy. It's pretty hard to not be engrossed by a person who is driving 2 luxury Mercedes, lived in 6,000 sq ft gorgeous semi-mansions (plural), and owned a 35 foot cigarette speed boat. He had it more than made. At any rate, we met, and he gave me the ABC's of the deal.

It was a challenging loan that just was not getting approved. The subject property was on a lake in Madison, and it was no shack. We are talking about a potential million-dollar loan. Dave was trying to simply build and flip it for huge profit. The profit really was there; $500k in profit. I saw it myself, crunching the comparables, recently sold. Those strips of homes were all sold to high-end clients from Madison, Milwaukee to Chicago and the suburbs.

I decided to put my own money into the deal. Here is when everything turned around for me. This was the decision that would completely change the playing field. I was cocky, confident, and thought I could get it done. However, the market was too tough, too tight. I will talk about being humbled by the experiences this market has offered builders, realtors and lenders.

I must have been on the 1-yard line so many times I thought I had it nailed down. But after 20+ banks later saying no, in different ways, I decided to walk away along with the tens of thousands of dollars I had spent getting the project started. The plan was to start building it for wholesale price. We could spend $10 and get $25 worth of construction because Dave was so darn efficient. If I spent $40k, we could easily get $85k of appraised value. If I could get $2 for almost every $1 I spent, and the banks were requiring 20% down, then the plan was to spend half that and make it look like 20% down.

The term 'making it look' sounds pretty devious. It wasn't exactly that. It's not like we were substituting quality or hiding anything. It's just how builders make money. A builder spends $250,000 on the materials and labor(including the land or tear down), and can walk away with a $100,000 profit, if he is good. The home doesn't have to be complete to earn that value. If a builder spends $1 on a home, he expects top turn a profit on it. It's all the same.

We were really creative, but it didn't matter. The deal was shot. I was in Miami, Fl for a few days just of R&R, just getting away from it all. Dave and I spoke and we just decided to walk away. It was just too much. The sleepless nights, the anxiety; it wasn't worth it anymore. The whole ordeal was almost a year, but it felt like three.

Dave and I wanted to flip properties. We'd start turning just one at a time, a safe pace, and slowly build our wealth. We both had the attitude of 'let's go, we can do it.' It's always been A to B for us. If it makes money and can be done, then let's do it. Pretty simple philosophy, without all the legwork. If you want to climb Mt. Everest, do you focus on the climb or being at the top? If you only focus on the climb, you'll likely talk yourself out of it. In contrast, if throughout your climb you're always imagining yourself at the top, well, you'll likely make it. If you don't, at least you gave it the best shot possible.

Dave eventually lost his license, his credit, his Mercedes. I was even there with him for some of it. We became friendly. Since Dave couldn't work on his own, he took on a position under another contractor. I knew the contractor and wasn't fond of him. Proper management, big thinking, and most of all, respect was not a part of his repertoire. I didn't really have a problem with the person. It's just that I knew Dave and I we are more similar in the way we thing. Here I was trying to do a few things with Dave when this other contractor just treated him like a puppet. He figured Dave would never be on his own so he might as well work him to death. Dave wasn't getting paid on time, if he was getting paid at all. It was awful. We were in a mouse maze with no way out.

We both felt that something had to be done. We didn't know exactly how or what, but whatever this situation was, it just wasn't right. We were both capable of the reaching the sky and here we were two inches above dirt pavement. Dave considered offering the other contractor 25% of everything he did on his own if he could jus use the credit. This is what got me thinking. I spent many nights, sleepless, trying to figure out the solution.

The other contractor was a straight line, just barely hovering above the ground, content with what he had. It was June or July and the company had probably made about $160k, year to date. But, Dave was doing all the work. It was Dave that was designing, meeting with the clients and reeling them all in, not the other putz.

One night I just thought to myself, maybe I can get my license. I had the credit, which Dave was aware of. We were buying some real estate with my credit anyway. It hit me like a wave of energy. As if I couldn't sleep for a week. I wanted to walk up to strangers and say hello because I was so excited. I was going to get my own license and we'd be home free.

Well, you can imagine what happened. A week later, after going through all the pre-licensing, I got the license. Dave and I came to the same agreement and we were both a little giddy. For Dave and I, we don't worry about how to get the business or how to make money. All we need is the door to open. That's what we get giddy about! We get excited by the opportunity!

About a month later, I had all the accounts setup, the website was looking good and Dave was just about done finishing all the jobs that were initially contracted under the other contractor. Dave was not just going to pick up and leave all the clients that he had met with and designed for. Screw the contractor; it wouldn't be right for those clients.

Within about 4 weeks of the company being born, we had 2 new home builds and 3 remodels; all without beginning to advertise. All the politics and red tape of working for someone else was gone. It's now wide open and very enthralling. We've taken on another 'partner/employee' to help out with some of the day-to-day work.

The building company, 24-7 Design Build, in Madison, WI is a productive entity that is rewarding everyday. Rather than go for the homerun like I did with the lake-home, this company produces reliable income every month. We've grown so quick and the sky really is the limit.

We will still be dabbling in real estate speculation. After all, it is a tremendous profit-making machine. However, the more stable remodeling and client new home build is really the core of the company.

I believe that anyone can do this. It's so damn simple a Neanderthal can do it. In fact, I see most other ventures as a scam compared to the simplicity of Wealth Innovative.

CHAPTER I

Introduction

Congratulations on your purchase of Wealth Innovative. In this guidebook, I will discuss the last 30+ years of our financial market and how it is has lead to the current day status. I will even provide personal accounts of my mortgage banking days, which will give you a blow by blow account of how we were lending behind closed doors. More specifically, the ups and downs of the last 8 or so years have brought us to not only one of the worst financial times, but some of the best investment opportunities. More than ever, products are cheap, businesses are discounted, real estate is being liquidated and builders need your help.

Never in a builder's lifetime would they extend their profit to another partner. However, they no longer have a choice. With all of the failures, and the remaining crumbles, several opportunities have fell through the cracks. The 2007- 2010 recession has provided us with exciting and ultra-profitable opportunities.

Without the current credit crisis, I would have never been presented with the opportunity to own a building company. This is one of the most crucial points of Wealth Innovative. I'll explain later how the current recession is unique and why this opportunity exists. Throughout the book, keep in mind that the recession and Wealth Innovative fit together like a lock & key.

The situation is sad with the many bankruptcies and builders going out of business. However, what it did do was finally open the door for people like you and I. Without a doubt, you'd never have this chance of a lifetime without the unfortunate help of the credit crisis. It would never happen because its entire foundation is based on restarting a failed builder. The builder was doing well, except something had to bring him down for us to even be in on the party. This model doesn't have anything to do with starting a brand new business from scratch. It's not even like purchasing a franchise. It's better! And I'll explain exactly how to do it. However, it's so crucial to understand why the opportunity even exists. The more you understand, the more you'll realize why this is a slam dunk.

Don't feel overwhelmed. The hard part is over. Many people are too afraid to consider other means of income. They feel that if they take a step to the right or left, they might fall completely off their track. The comfort-zone is most often the demise of entrepreneurship. Moreover, consider the trends among the wealthy during a recession.

The key to being a successful, well to do business-man is the ability to see the big picture and maintain perspective. The wealthy understand that recessions are cyclical. The 2007 recession will come and go. You can bet there will be another one, and another, and another. Businesses will fail for different reasons. Each recession or failure is completely different. However, there is one thing that will always remain the same. Those with perspective will thrive on all of it. In fact, todays and yesterdays rich most likely got fat on the failure of something else. It's not like every wealthy person came up with some mind-blowing idea or innovation. But, what they did do was pull the trigger when it counted. Let's now explain it in more detail.

Whether the recession affects stocks, homes or commodities, most people retreat. They run away from it like a house on fire. The wealthy thrive in these times because the prices drop on everything. The competition dwindles away as well, and those investors get to cherry pick the best available funds. Imagine shutting the lights on the world for 2 years. Switch them back on and the rich are now richer. They now own three times as much and are making 10 times the money. This is exactly what is happening all around you.

The opportunities are everywhere. How many $2.5 billion building in Manhattan being liquidated for $1billion. The bank worth $15 billion being purchased for $2 billion. The house down the street once worth $500k being dissolved for half. The credit card companies upping their rates and minimal payments. Seize the opportunity to grab more!

During these times, the people on the bottom need the people on the top even more. They are less viable and more vulnerable. This is nature, survival of the fittest, whatever you'd like to call it. Among all animals or humans, when one displays defeat or weakness, those with power smell blood and get hungrier.

I like to compare owning a business or real estate as having a share of the limited seeds in circulation. A seed may not look like much until it's planted and harvested. However, what was once a small seed can grow into a monstrous tree. Moreover, how much does a seed cost in comparison to a grown plant, flower or tree. It takes time and effort to grow that tree and you end up paying for it. The problem is that unlike plants, it's harder to purchase companies at the seed level…until a recession comes along!

Who ever dreamed of shares of Fannie Mae or General Motors plummeting under $1? In fact, GM is off the Dow Jones trading block. It's all preposterous. However, just like any other stock trade, when these company stocks rise back up to $40/share, the people who accept the fact that these tides are cyclical will turn ridiculous profits. And the people who didn't pull the trigger will once again complain that they 'should have seen it coming'.

It is common belief that getting in on the bottom floor is almost impossible today. You have the major established companies that just keep growing more and more. I just explained how these companies purchase more of the 'limited 'seeds'. However, this philosophy applies to everybody! The illustration of 'limited seeds' is actually a very basic business model used for thousands of years. Think about it; GE and Microsoft didn't come onto the scene with millions. They all started with one seed.

Every single company or person starts with one seed. Now, it's your turn. I'll show you how easy it is to start your own seed….. let's call it a company from here on out.

Would you believe that I started my own successful building company in less than two months? Not only did I get the company up and running, but it has injected a wealth of income into my life. It's exciting and rewarding, but most of all, the sky is the limit. If you think I'm going to stop there, you're dreaming. It's easier than ever to turn one into five.

In the chapters ahead I will explain how I generated the Wealth Innovative business model. The opportunity to be in this position has been a special work in progress since 2002. I will highlight how the evolution of the last 6 to 7 years has produced this incredible opportunity. I'll include snippets of the last 30 years to really demonstrate my point. You'll slowly recognize how the very basic economic picture I provide applies to the business model. First, let's review the advantages of owning your own business.

CHAPTER II

Owning your own Business

Owning your own business can seem like a pain in the butt. Having to trust managers and employees could be an issue. What about bringing in enough business to pay the rent and business expenses? Where do you even come up with the money to put down? Therefore, most of the time, affordability is the overpowering reason for apprehension.

You can disregard just about every concern with the business model I will outline. For now, let's focus on the advantages of owning your own business:

- **Years of hard work can result in wealth not unemployment**

- **For the self-employed, just about everything is a tax write-off**

- **You will have the ability and time to help others**

- **You will have more time to spend with your family**

- **You will have more self-esteem**

- **You will have much more freedom**

- **You're in control of your own fate!**

Here is my personal perspective: when I look around at the friends and colleagues I have known and worked with, the happiest and most satisfied people are those that own their own businesses. They have the most freedom, even more than the top CEOs. These people answer to nobody and they call their own shots.

Many CEO's are on top of the world. They worked hard, but moreover, are **smart**. It is more due to their brilliant strategic decisions. They made a lot of small decisions that added up as well. They truly deserve their success.

As an employee you can dedicate many years of your life to a company, only to find yourself out of a job due to situations totally out of your control. Management changes, mergers, acquisitions, downsizing and outsourcing all have a tendency to force sudden and unexpected change.

Consider the environment of the self-employed. If you own your own business, you might still face adversity. However, it is all within your control. If success was all up to you, would you let yourself down? In the real world, success is not up to you. What if a company is not hiring? How about a supervisor or boss that you just don't work well with?

Every decision a company makes benefits the owners or founders. If they are hiring, firing, downsizing, changing pay, altering the colors of their logo….you can bet it all has to satisfy the people on top. You are not in control and don't have a say in these decisions, unless of course your idea benefits the Board and makes them lots of money. When owning your own business, you become the man or woman on top.

There are over 1,000,000 new businesses started every year. 40% of them fail in the first year. Another 40% fail before year five. So the odds are against you. However, there are ways to beat the odds. The success rate for franchises, for example, is much, much higher. Approximately 50% or more of the franchises make it past five years.

The key to success is the "Turn Key" business. If your business truly has to start from the ground floor up, it will be tough. With Wealth Innovative you will see how you are adopting an already successful business and owning it. You won't believe how simplistic it is. When I realized what it took to start my company, I was always wondering what I was missing. Unlike a new business or franchise, a building company is 95% up to the talent of the builder. You'll understand that it's not about being in the right location, or worrying about a competitor moving into the building across the street.

Owning your own business really does allow you to set your own schedule and enjoy your vacations. Independent contractors of real estate, such as realtors and builders, may take a month long vacation over the Christmas holiday. They do it because they can! Your first response might be, 'wait a minute, almost every store from Wal-Mart to the local grocery store is always open'. Sure, they're always open because the owners hire employees to keep it open all that time. You ever see the owner or founder walking the aisles on Thanksgiving? These people are on a beach in Miami, on the internet using their top of the line laptop, to monitor their ever growing bank account.. Everybody on the executive level just pays other people time and a half to work the holidays. Time and a half? The owners are making time x 200. Sure, they'll give you your time and a half any day.

It may be tough to accept the fact that if you're not in, you're out. It's an old cliché, but it's true. All those conversations and decisions about how to run the world really do take place behind closed doors. These people spend 1% of their time getting it set up while you spend 40% of your time running it for them. Of course it could take 6 months, or even 2 years to get any business set up, but not a turn-key contractor business like Wealth Innovative!

The Wealth Innovative model obviously revolves around the home building trade. The building trade is closely tied to the economy, the real estate market and credit. One cannot really thrive without the other and the home remodeling/building market is no different.

Before we break down why this business is so profitable, it's important to realize how we even have a shot like this. For one, you can start a new business or franchise whenever you like. However, this business is unique and only very recently available. For anyone like you and I, who are outside the circle of the building trade, very specific events had to occur for the door to open.

The better understanding you have of the real estate market and how it has led to our current state of the economy, the more you'll appreciate Wealth Innovative. You really need to accept the fact that this was never available before and also won't last forever.

CHAPTER III

Market Failure

Sure, it is imperative to understand how the opportunity for an average entrepreneur to own a building company came to fruition. Again, keep in mind that many nasty things had to occur for you to be in this position to prosper. One must be humble and appreciate the history of the market. The individuals in the lending, real estate and building trades have endured quite a bit. They have had to reinvent themselves and perhaps look at other avenues for income. Therefore, imagine being in their position. Jumping into the stream apathetically will earn you no points.

Personally, I like my piece of pie. I am in favor of the idea of Capitalism because I believe that if you work hard, or come up with an ingenious idea, you get rewarded for it. Don't get too excited. I am in favor of the notion of Capitalism, however, not necessarily what our current idea of Capitalism is.

According to Wikipedia, the definition of Capitalism is : an economic and social system in which capital, the non-labor factors of production (also known as the means of production), is privately controlled; labor, goods and capital are traded in markets; and profits distributed to owners or invested in technologies and industries. Essentially, it means that trade is not partially or wholly government controlled as in the cases of Socialism and Communism. In Lehman's terms, it means any citizen of a Capitalist country can put in the time and claim their own private stake in a business, a product, or an idea. It originated in the 16th century, but really grew in the late 19th century as industrialization began to boom, also know as the Industrial Revolution.

Recessions have occurred throughout the history of modern economics. Capitalism is not to blame for the recessions. However, you could make the argument that it was a catalyst for the most recent recession of 2007. Without money hungry Wall Street banks, investors and politicians, we'd still have an economic decline in the real estate market, but, it would never be the rollercoaster that it is been. The National Bureau of Economic Research defines economic recession as a significant decline in the economic activity spread across the economy, lasting more than a few months. As familiar as we are with the economic recession, the United States is not the only country to suffer from them.

The United States suffered its first recession between 1797 and 1800. It was called the panic of 1797, and it was primarily caused by the deflating effects of the Bank of England as they crossed the ocean to American soil. This disrupted commercial real estate markets in the U.S. Britain's economy was in a strained state already, because it was fighting France in the French Revolutionary War at the time. This is just one example of how the effects of recession on one country can travel quickly to another. Economists all agree that what effects one country, especially a key country, will affect the rest of the world in at least one way, shape, or form, before the recession is over.

The next confirmed recession occurred in the years between 1807 and 1814, and was called the Depression of 1807. This depression was primarily caused by the Embargo Act of 1807, signed into effect by President Thomas Jefferson. This act destroyed a good part of the shipping related industries, and it was fought hard by the Federalists, who allowed smuggling to take effect in New England as a result of the Act.

The Panic of 1819 soon followed. This was considered the first major financial crisis to unveil itself to the relatively new U.S. economy. This panic brought with it widespread foreclosures, failing banks, huge unemployment rates, and a gigantic slump in manufacturing and agriculture that caused havoc among Americans. This recession also marked the end of great economic expansion that had taken place following the War of 1812.

Economic recessions in America continued with the Panic of 1837. This recession can really be attributed to failing banks, and to the lack of confidence people had in paper currency, which was becoming popular at the time. Banks stopped paying out in gold and silver, which really took its toll on American confidence.

The Panic of 1857 followed not long after. With the failure of the Ohio Life Insurance and Trust Company (which at the time was one of the biggest in the United States) came the explosion of a European confidence bubble in the U.S. This greatly affected the railroads and U.S. banks, causing over 5,000 businesses in America to fail in the first year of the panic alone. Unemployment rose, and protest meetings became popular.

Recessions continued to plague not only America, but the rest of the world as well. Considered part of the natural cycle of the modern economic system, no one can really escape recession in the long run. Countries like Germany, the U.K., China, and Japan have all had trouble with recessions. In fact, economists say that Germany is in for what might be the biggest recession in all of German history not too far down the road. Japanese economic recession has also played a huge part in their history. Japanese recessions, just like economic recessions in America, can be linked to the dreadful cycle of imbalanced inflation, money supply, and interest rates that keep things in balance, rolling, and functioning properly.

TIMELINE:

The events of the past 30-40 years has led to the current state affairs. The economy of a Capitalist country like the United States is a never ending balancing act. A spike in the economy will eventually prompt the Fed to take action. Any prolonged bear market will cause an inflation. An inflation could lead to a recession. The 2007 recession was created because of the Real Estate boom. The boom was caused from a prior slide. That slide was caused from the tech boom aftermath. It goes on and on and on.

Wealth Innovative is simply a product of the last 40 years. Below, is a timeline which boldly illustrates the see-saw economy we live in. These are the actual newspaper titles and abstracts.

Rollercoaster of the 1970's

FEBRUARY 1, 1974

Los Angeles Times

"U.S. WILL TOTTER ON BRINK OF RECESSION, NIXON AIDES SAY"

Inflation and unemployment will get worse, not better, in 1974 and the economy will totter at the threshold of recession for much of the year, President Nixon's chief economic advisers said today.

JANUARY 13, 1976

New York Times

"ALARM ON CITBANK AND CHASE SETS OFF HEAVY TRADING"

Bank stocks sold off sharply yesterday and then recovered most of their losses in the wake of weekend reports that the First National City Bank and the Chase Manhattan Bank were on a "problem list" compiled by the Comptroller of the Currency

DECEMBER 16, 1978

Los Angeles Times

"FED'S MILLER AND BURNS DIFFER ON PROSPECTS OF '79 RECESSION"

Federal Reserve Chairman G. William Miller and his predecessor, Arthur F. Burns, differed Friday over whether a recession would occur in 1979 and whether a downturn would help dampen inflation.

JANUARY 5, 1981

New York Times

"REPUBLICAN SENATORS SAY ECONOMY IS TOP PRIORITY"

The incoming Congress should concentrate on "getting the economy on its feet" rather than on such issues as abortion, school prayer and busing to achieve integration, two Republican Senators said today. "We've got to be more flexible and work together," said Senator Orrin G. Hatch of Utah, who is considered a conservative.

Microsoft, Atari, IBM prompts new age

SEPTEMBER 19, 1982

Chicago Tribune

"DEMOCRATS PLAN TO PLUG ECONOMY INTO HIGH-TECH"

House Democrats outlined Saturday a $40 billion to $45 billion a year plan to move the American economy into a high-technology age with a crash program for training workers, increasing invest

DECEMBER 29, 1984

Miami Herald

"NEW STRENGTH FOR ECONOMY IS SEEN IN '85"

Government statistics released Friday indicated that the U.S. economy may be greeting the new year with renewed strength, but that it would be even stronger if it weren't for the sky-rocketing U.S. dollar. The government's index of leading indicators, a barometer of future economic activity, went up 1.3 percent in November. It was the strongest increase in 10 months.

Another Slide

JUNE 7, 1987

Washington Post

"NOMINEE ALAN GREENSPAN ON THE U.S. ECONOMY, GLOBAL POLICY AND THE FED"

"Fed policy remains extremely accommodative, but the easing which began last April appears to have been completed. . . . The pause in Fed policy is consistent with comments by Vice Chairman {Manuel H.} Johnson that this was desirable in view of signs that economic activity might be firming. He also noted increased concern about inflation, as evident in the rise in bond yields."

FEBRUARY 21, 1990

Boston Globe

"A PUSH FOR THE ECONOMY"

Conventional wisdom has it that Wall Street follows the economy. Boom times mean bull markets. Downturns raise hob with stock prices. Alan Greenspan told Congress yesterday that the economy was past danger of a recession and would grow modestly this year. That, according to conventional wisdom, should have made Wall Street moderately happy. Instead, prices dropped sharply -- and with good reason.

Beginning of an Upward Swing

FEBRUARY 20, 1992

USA Today

"GREENSPAN SEES ECONOMY COMING BACK"

The Fed expects consumer prices to rise 3% to 3.5% this year, vs. 3.1% last year. That looks like no improvement. But [Alan Greenspan] pointed out that last year, inflation was held in check because of a one-time sharp drop in energy prices.

AUGUST 17, 1994

New York Times

"FEDERAL RESERVE RAISES KEY RATES TO COOL ECONOMY"

The Federal Reserve raised the interest rates it controls today, hoping to prevent the economy's continuing strength from leading to inflation but making it more expensive for Americans to borrow money.

MARCH 27, 1996

New York Times

"GREENSPAN CITES GROWING ECONOMY: FED KEEPS U.S. RATES UNCHANGED"

The committee met for less than three hours and adjourned without announcing any action or issuing a formal statement. This had been widely expected after conflicting statistics earlier this year were followed by a surge in employment, indicating that the Fed did not need to take action to spur the economy.

Tech Boom Running Wall Street

MARCH 19, 1999

Chicago Tribune

"ECONOMY AND STOCKS ON A ROLL"

When the nation's top banker, Alan Greenspan, tried to take some sizzle out of the U.S. stock market in December 1996 by warning against "irrational exuberance," the Dow Jones industrial average stood at 6,437 and the economic expansion had just turned 5 1/2 years old.

Economy already on downward trend

SEPTEMBER 4, 2001

Washington Post

"BUSH SAYS HE IS 'CONCERNED' OVER ECONOMY"

[Bush] is shifting his focus in response to a drop in consumer confidence, which fell last month to the lowest level since April, a skittish stock market and slackened business activity. The budget surplus has eroded much of the money that Bush had been counting on in his plans to reshape education policy, boost military spending and reform Social Security and Medicare.

9/11 Aftermath

FEBRUARY 11, 2002

Fox News

"GREENSPAN: ECONOMY STILL FACES RISKS"

Greenspan, making his first public comments on the economy since the Fed last cut interest rates on Dec. 11, said there are "tentative indications" that the economic slump could be drawing to a close, but he said those signals at present are far from conclusive.

OCTOBER 2, 2002

USA Today

"GORE URGES PRESIDENT TO FOCUS ON ECONOMY"

Former vice president Al Gore on Wednesday urged President Bush to put the same intense focus on the U.S. economy that he has on the prospective war with Iraq. He said the nation's economy is "in big trouble" and the White House prescriptions are "really failing us."

JANUARY 4, 2003

Times Online

"SCEPTICS QUESTION BUSH'S $300 BILLION BOOST TO ECONOMY"

Mr. Bush will use an address in Chicago to spell out measures worth up to $300 billion over the next ten years, the centrepiece of which is expected to be a reduction in the tax paid on dividends.

SEPTEMBER 4, 2003

USA Today

"BUSH SAYS ECONOMY IS RECOVERING"

President Bush, facing growing concerns and criticism about the economy, expressed optimism Thursday that the country is heading in the right direction — toward "greater prosperity and more jobs.

REAL ESTATE BOOM BEGINS

JULY 20, 2004

Bloomberg

"WELLS FARGO 2ND QUARTER RISES 12% ON LENDING"

Wells Fargo and Co., the fifth-largest U.S. bank, said second-quarter profit increased 12 percent as it boosted consumer lending and earned more fees from services including insurance and managing investments for individuals.

JANUARY 15, 2005

New York Times

"IN REAL ESTATE, WHAT GOES UP KEEPS RISING"

These increases, even in the face of sluggish job growth on Wall Street and an overall economy that lags the nation's, indicate that "the rules of real estate have changed" as several factors have combined to keep pushing prices upward, said Jonathan J. Miller, president of Miller Samuel Inc. Several years of historically low mortgage rates, coupled with continued migration of new residents to the city, have kept demand high, and the market hot.

BEGINNING OF THE END

MARCH 8, 2006

FORBES

"BEN BERNANKE WARNS LOCAL BANKS REGARDING REAL ESTATE LOANS"

Alan Greenspan, *that former Federal Reserve chairman-turned- big-ticket diarist, was in some ways a stick-in-the-mud: At the height of the real-estate boom, he kept reminding everyone that many investors might be overextended, reserving specific caveats for Fannie Mae and Freddie Mac. The government-backed mortgage giants, he warned, had portfolios that may have grown too vast.*

JUNE 28, 2007

MSNBC

"ECONONMY GROWTH WEAKEST IN OVER 4 YEARS"

The economy limped ahead at just a 0.7 percent pace in the first quarter, the slowest in more than four years, as some businesses clamped down on spending given uncertainties about the severity of the housing slump.

BUBBLE-BURST

NOVEMBER 9, 2008

YAHOO!

"TRIAL OF EX BEAR STEARNS EXEC GOES TO JURY"

Pay and venue were the focus of a jury's early deliberations on Monday in the trial of two former Bear Stearns hedge fund managers accused of fraud over dealings in mortgage-backed securities early in the financial crisis.

DECEMBER 2, 2008

Los Angeles Times

"RECESSION COULD LAST INTO 2010"

The economy's yearlong downturn, officially declared a recession Monday, could last well into next year or even beyond, challenging the government to devise new responses as traditional methods show limited results.

APRIL 14, 2009

Market Watch

"ECONOMY MUST BE BUILT ON ROCK, NOT SAND: OBAMA SAYS"

In what the White House is billing as a major address on the economy at Georgetown University, Obama said his economic policies are designed to help the economy recover now and build a stronger economy for the long haul, one that isn't built on quick profits, too much debt, and stagnant wages.

The recession of 2007 is a bit similar to that of the Savings and Loan Crisis in the 1980's, when 745 savings and loan associations went bankrupt. The deregulation of the S&L's gave way to imprudent lending. It was a combination of events that led to the breakdown. Because of the deregulation, thrifts were competing against one another for the best CD rates and returns on investments. If you listen to children argue they obviously miss the big picture. The S&L's were just going back and forth saying in a high pitched voice 'No, we have the best rates in town'.

If an S&L was offering 5% return on a CD, they'd obviously have to come up with the money from somewhere to pay the investor. Actually returning those high yields to clients could only derive from another investment that would earn them that return and, hopefully, more. Turns out the whole operation was just a borrow from Peter to pay Paul type of tactic that resulted in disaster.

The Tax Reform Act of 1986 (26 U.S.C. § 469) significantly reduced the returns on many investments. It was pretty idiotic to pass such a law after all the investments were already made. In an attempt to regulate lending, the bottom fell out and eventually led to the 1990 recession as well. We've been playing catch-up ever since. You heard that right; we've been playing catch-up ever since to recoup the losses.

The banking conglomerates have been chasing their tails for 3 decades now. I do not believe Capitalism is inherently evil. It worked before and it can work just fine. The issue was the **deregulation** of derivatives and lending (which will cover very soon).

As opposed to yesterdays Capitalism, the problem with today's Capitalism is people are committing themselves to everything that should breed success, but instead find themselves walking the same tight rope despite their best efforts. Whether you're a small business owner, a teacher, a firefighter; it all doesn't matter anymore. We've turned into a regime in which the extremely few powers on top have complete control over the rest. That's not Capitalism.

The true idea of Capitalism is very inspiring. The true idea of Capitalism is what America used to be about. The idea of 'life, liberty, and the pursuit of happiness' is why my father came here in 1955. He knew that if he put his mind to something, he'd be equally rewarded. In so many countries, the ceiling is so low that if you worked 24 hours a day, you'd still wind up with scraps. Guess what? That's what Capitalism has become.

The United States of America has been a Capitalist country for some time. In fact, just about as long as we've been independent. It's pretty hard to incorporate life in the early 20th century into this discussion because you might remember the two World Wars. However, life in the 1950's and 1960's was not all that bad. More of the pie was spread out rather than the notorious top 1% owning more than the bottom 95% combined. Something must have happened. Changes must have been made.

The Capitalism even before the Oil Embargo of 1973 was very different. Most work was kept here, meaning, American companies employed American workers to produce product. Most Americans aspired to own a Ford, a Chevy, even a Cadillac, if they were lucky. However, in 1973, the Organization of Arab Petroleum Exporting Countries (OAPEC), declared it would stop or limit oil to the US.

The Oil Embargo was a response to the US' support of the Israeli Military, in particular, during the Yom Kippur war. Any ally of the US was affected by the boycott as well, which led to a global recession. The world was mercy to the limited supply of crude oil. The event sparked the production of more gas efficient cars, which the Japanese had 3 legs up on. The muscle cars and their big block engines of the 1950's and 1960's would slowly die.

Michael Moore recently made a movie called "Capitalism', in which he pretty much abolishes Capitalism for good. He believes we should completely change the economic DNA of this country. Of course, that's impossible. Moreover, it's unnecessary. It would be great if we could divide the country into two; have one half run as a Capitalist entity and the other as a Socialist or Communist economy and just see what happens. Well, that's exactly what happened in Germany after WWII. They didn't just divide the county in half, they built a friggin wall to separate the two, i.e., the Berlin Wall.

Within two years after WWII, the capital of Berlin was split between the Soviets and the remaining occupying powers of France, Britain, and the United States. Joseph Stalin, then the Soviet leader, built up a protective belt of Soviet controlled nations, called the Eastern Bloc. Property and industry was nationalized in the East German zone. After Stalin instituted a Western blockage in 1948, the Allied powers began the infamous "Berlin airlift", which supplied West Berlin with food and other supplies.

October 7, 1949, East Germany was officially under the Soviet regime and their communist ideology. Western Germany was adopted as a Western Capitalist country with an injection of some Socialist principles. You can imagine what happened next. The majority of those living in the Eastern Bloc aspired to move to West Germany. Most of the people who risked their lives crossing the border were professionally skilled and educated people like engineers, physicians, teachers, and lawyers.

Now ask yourself, why did so many people migrate to this county, on boats, from their homelands? True Capitalism and the 'American Dream' is what makes our land so special. When immigrants crossed the Berlin Wall, or migrated to the US, they weren't hosed by their employers or controlled by massive credit card debt and upside down mortgages. All these people came to this country and truly found a better life. But greed, not Capitalism, is why those jobs were eventually take away and shipped them to China or Thailand.

The industry to be hit most by greedy capitalists would be the garment business. Fashion Ave in New York used to buzz day and night with activity. Today, you'd be hard-pressed to find a label that uses American workers.

Once a company is incorporated, and made public, shareholders want more, more, and more profits. You can't charge $1,000 for a pair of $100 jeans because nobody will buy them. Instead, ship the work oversees where people will work for $1/week. That's how you turn more profit.

Capitalism is a great idea, but, it can easily morph into its ugly cousin, Greed. The garment business is no stranger. If you think paying Americans to stitch your major American label jeans will make them even more expensive, you're wrong. Instead, it'll cost $15 to make a pair of jeans sold for $150. However, if the company pays employees 'more' to make the jeans, it will then appear that the company is losing money. Shareholders then panic because their stock is dropping, therefore they sell, which then seriously jeopardizes the integrity of the company. Everybody wants to stick their hands into the pockets of other companies and make money. Once that happens, the original founder of the company loses all power. He/she/they must now answer to quarterly reports.

As far as the current collapse is concerned, you can point the finger at the deregulation of derivative swaps. It's actually all been about 30 years in the making. In financial markets, the term derivatives is used to refer to a group of instruments that derive their value from some underlying commodity or market. Early evidence of these types of instruments can be traced back to ancient Greece. Aristotle related a story about how the Greek philosopher Thalus profited handsomely from an option-type agreement around the 6th century b.c. According to the story, one-year prior, Thalus forecast the next olive harvest would be an exceptionally good one. As a poor philosopher, he did not have many financial resources at hand, but he used what he had to place a deposit on the local olive presses. Thalus secured the rights to the presses at a relatively low rate and when the harvest proved to be abundant the demand for the presses soared.

The first swap agreements were executed by the Salomon Brothers in London in 1981, while equity derivatives, based on underlying stock indices, began to emerge in the late 1980's. Credit default products are the most commonly traded credit derivative product and include unfunded products such as credit default swaps. Derivatives are very complicated, incredibly risky, unmonitored bank gambling. A Wall Street genius will write the algorithm (a mathematical formula), which looks like a physics equation out of Einstein's head. It's basically the most complex sports bet you can imagine. Any bet with a Vegas casino bookie is not too difficult. It could be an over/under, or a spread, or possibly some variation. These derivatives are the same thing, except they are betting on real world events that are a thousand times more complicated, and a million times more dangerous.

Derivatives became incredibly popular in the mid 1990's. If you recall, communism was finally over, no more cold war, and politics really started to have an effect on banking. Some feel the fall of the Berlin Wall was the beginning of the new world we live in now. Time magazine even recently published a special edition piece titled '1989'. The country went through a recession in the early 1990's when Clinton took over. We were sill suffering from the 1987 real estate crash, which was inspired in part by the Savings and Loan crisis.

The derivative market was worth somewhere around $27 Trillion in the mid 1990's. That is a lot of money, right? Well, by 2008, The Bank for International Settlements estimates that outstanding derivatives total $592 trillion (4). Now you get the picture of how grave and global the collapse we endured. Banks were putting bundles of money into derivatives that invested in anything and everything; technology, oil, medical advancements, etc. The S&P and NASDAQ were exploding because of bank investments. With returns of 40-50%, things looked great and Alan Greenspan assured Washington that our economy was never healthier. Tons of money was invested and the economy swelled to an exciting level of activity.

It was absolutely insane to go against the grain and ever think something was off. However, the truth of the matter was that all these derivatives were deregulated, which means nobody was even allowed to monitor or audit the investments. Not the SEC, not the government, NOBODY. It was considered a 'black box' investment. Investors threw their money into funds and had no idea how they were earning 50%. Come to think of it, why would they care?

There were very few people who would challenge the system and warn congress of the inherent danger of deregulated derivative swaps. The US Commodity Futures Trading Commission had no power over Wall Street. All the banks were making secret deals with billions of dollars that only a few knew about. Just that in itself sounds a little shady to me. It sounds like a helpless gambler who has to sneak in bets while nobody is watching.

The real estate crash was just another form of a deregulated derivative disaster. Instead of technology stocks, banks were betting on the real estate market. It was the last straw. The last card in the whole house of cards and it all caved in. In 2008, Alan Greenspan admitted to Congress that he was wrong. After 40 years in the business and practicing finance the same way for all that time, Greenspan came clean to Congress when he said that his 'outlook of the world was false'. The entire panel was awe-struck. For heavens sake, this guy was the Chairman of the Federal Reserve for almost 20 years! Throughout the late 1990's crash and 2006 warning of a bubble-burst, it was Alan Greenspan that we looked to for reassurance that everything was to be ok. The admission was way too little and way too late. Wall Street's nightmare was very real.

I believe the person on top should earn the most. After all, it is he or she that produced the opportunities for the rest in the first place. However, for the top guy to make 98% and the rest making the other 2% is wrong.

The small business-owner makes Capitalism work. Earning a few million dollars a year is a blessing. However, stealing from the lower class to give to the upper class is a huge mistake. The only way Capitalism works is to share the wealth. I'm not talking about giving up money earned. But the idea of a democracy has failed when 5% of the people have 100% of the power. Requiring employees to work twice as hard for half as much so the people on top can flourish just doesnt work.

Unfortunately, this is the country that we live in. The rules currently favor the people on top and you have to be blind not to realize it. Everyone from the CEO's of banks and credit cards are all in on it. As you are reading this, they are making money on you!

Here's a little tidbit: Have you wondered why most credit card bills are mailed from South Dakota or Delaware? In the 1980's, banks could only charge a defined ceiling on their credit card interest rates. The rates were all around 11% and all states were regulated. The governor presiding over South Dakota, with specifically Sioux Falls in mind, was pressured to bring business back to the community. The people were suffering and no traffic was coming through. The city looked like the setting of a 1930's movie.

When South Dakota deregulated the interest rates on credit cards you can imagine what happened next. All of a sudden the governor is having face-to-face meetings with the CEO's of Chase and Bank of America. These executives in $4,000 suits came from their skyscrapers in Manhattan to a little bungalow in South Dakota to meet with the governor. In that instance, the credit card conglomerate was born, giving birth to entire banks such as MBNA. The accumulation of consumer debt gaining interest at over 20% solely gave rise to several billion dollar entities. Yep, your debt is paying for a whole city to prosper.

Now, the modern financial crisis started to take shape post 9/11. In 2002-2003 if you remember, was the tremendous real estate 'refi-boom'. After 9/11, the economy was in shambles. The government used some scare tactics to completely take the spotlight off the banking industry. White collar crimes were incredibly prevalent and becoming a serious risk. Recall the Enron scandal or when Bernard Madoff started his Ponzi scheme? However, after 9/11, none if it mattered anymore. The country was scared stiff and resources were all thrown in one basket. We were going to blow the hell out of anything that moved.

Airlines were losing money because people didn't fly. We were convinced that if there were 19 hijackers, there must be 190,000 more. It actually was not the case. We were not battling entire countries like in WWII. Moreover, it took those terrorist morons years to put together one single attack. 9/11 was horrible and we were trained to believe that it could happen a dozen more times. I'm positive the FBI and other intelligence agencies have intercepted attacks on our country, and we should thank them for it. However, in comparison to the genuine Soviets threats of the 1950's, these piece of crap terrorists are nobodies.

The Soviets were engaging in visible nuclear bomb tests in the 1950's. We knew they had a stellar Navy and Air Force. Soviets rocketed a man into space before us and we had cause for concern. JFK challenged our military to land on the moon before 1970. It wasn't because he wanted something cool to watch on TV. It was all about conquering space in response to a genuine threat. How in the heck can you compare the Soviet power to some morons who had to hi-jack our own jets because they don't even have any of their own? Give me a break.

At any rate, post 9/11 is really when the banks loosened. However, this was obviously not our first financial crisis. Since the Reagan administration, the country has thrived on bank success. When banks lose money, the economy slows. We live in a Capitalist country, which mean the country revolves around the small business. Sure, we have the large corporations, but, the real backbone is comprised of all the small businesses. Your local doctor, plumber, dentist, coffee shops, theaters, restaurants, and builders! Where do small and local businesses get Capital to start and thrive on; banks! Therefore, Capitalism inherently feeds off banks.

The country had suffered an economic crisis just a few years before 9/11 with the technology (.com) bubble burst. The market took a tremendous hit when the .com boom blew up to tremendous proportions, and then fell back down to earth. We couldn't go through the same thing, therefore, President Bush encouraged the country to keep spending.

The interest rates that banks offer are closely tied to the 10 Year Treasury. The Treasury is an AAA Credit rating investment; it is bullet-proof. Perchance you've heard the saying 'if you want a sure thing, buy bonds', because it's true. There is no risk at all, which also means there is minimal return. The mortgage interest rates are typically 50-150 basis points (%) above the Treasury for a reason. First of all, the spread will vary all the time. You cannot simply predict the mortgage rates by adding a fixed number to the Treasury. The increased interest rate offsets the risk of the paper. The higher the rate, the higher the risk, thereby offsets the risk. You'll notice that a 4-unit home, or a subprime loan has much higher rates. Sure, the bank is making money. However, the academic reason is to offset risk. The financial purpose is to collect money. Consider how you would lend $10 to a trustworthy friend vs. one that is a little shaky?

I became a mortgage banker after the refinance-boom. As a mortgage banker, I was permitted to lend unconsciously to borrowers. The bank cartels came up with a new drug and gave it to bankers like myself to push on the streets. I didn't know what was really in the drug. As long as it had a major bank name on the box, it must be safe, right?!

We were all convinced homeowners were sitting on a pile of cash, i.e., their home. It was encouraged to borrow money. After all, the rates were pushed low to boost the economy. One way to lend more money was to make money cheap. Borrowers were persuaded to consolidate all their debt including their credit cards, car loans, student loans, and medical payments. When money is cheap, people borrow. When people borrow, people spend more. It was cheaper than ever to take out equity lines, car loans or anything else extended via credit. Making money cheap is one way to boost borrowing and spending.

Making money cheap for those who are worthy of borrowing that capital is typically safe. However, loosening lending practices is really what sent the country into a frenzy. The Fannie Mae and Freddie Mac guidelines, for example, are precise measurements enforced to maintain responsible borrowing. When those guidelines were thinned out, we fell into the Savings and Loan trap of imprudent lending again. Bank vaults were essentially kept open 24 hours a day. Anybody could come in and take what they wanted.

Money was still pretty cheap, but all the guidelines were somehow arbitrarily stretched. As a banker, I didn't know why or how they were loosened. It all came from the top executives, passed down to regional managers who then informed local supervisors.

The banks wanted more, more, and more. The people like myself on the mortgage banker level were not told a peep about the small print and the underlying motivation. They were getting us drunk but never really telling us what was in the Kool-Aid.

The banks couldn't get enough. So, in addition to the already loose loans being written, we tapped into another well; subprime. Subprime loans were not government backed like Conforming loans. Instead, subprime was completely funded through private investors, for example, Wall Street banks.

The minimum required credit scores were becoming lower and lower. The amount of money you needed to earn became less and less. Banks use a calculation called debt-to-income ratio. They calculate your income….multiply that number by a certain percentage, subtract your debt…..what is left determines what you can afford. The percentage they once used was approximately 36%, a very conservative and safe number. The calculation is like a contingency plan.

For argument sake, if you make $100, and have no debt at all, the bank will let you use about $36 of it toward a mortgage payment. Considering that you have groceries, entertainment, car payment, clothes, emergency reserves, the contingency plan is a very prudent guideline. The problem was that the debt-to-income ratio changed literally overnight. The ratio soon became 40%, 45%, 50%, 65%. All of a sudden, every $1 you made got you more. The drugs just got cheaper! I've seen loans approved where the debt ratio was in the low 70%!! Keep in mind it was once half that!

The deregulation of lending allowed this to happen. Mind you, a 70% debt to income ratio might not be a bad idea. However, it must be monitored. You cannot offer it to everybody. Regulating lending doesn't imply that banks can't offer custom financing. Regulation does not imply installing super-strict rules. It's not as if you have to put all your money down to purchase a home. It also certainly has nothing to do with the interest rates skyrocketing. Lastly, regulating lending will not result in a boring selection of mortgage products to choose from.

Regulating banking will just refrain banks from running wild with no oversight. The institutions can still employ creative financing. The product would simply need a final review from mommy and daddy in order to offer it to you. If the FDA did not regulate pharmaceuticals, can you imagine the crap that would be offered on the shelf at Walgreens? The medication sold on the shelves at your local pharmacy is regulated. Does that mean the choices are limited? We have 100 drugs in all shapes, sizes, names and colors for every darn problem you can imagine. If you don't know what hurts, they probably have something for that too!

Typically, a product that is publicly available is simply scrubbed and reviewed carefully. My experience at a Phase I FDA Pharmaceutical Research clinic after college was the embodiment of strict regulation. In those clinics we took better care of the volunteers than they might care for themselves. In that case, all we're doing is regulating that specific industry. Sometimes, there are side effects that all the doctors and scientists didn't discover, and unfortunately were revealed only after the medication's release. However, how often does that happen? Moreover, if it does happen, even that scenario is regulated with immediate predetermined steps!

Admitting that nothing will be perfect is a good start because in the event of a mishap, at least we'll be prepared. Banking in the US has been running without a safety net for quite some time. We've been operating under the illusion that banking is built with some immune system that will just fight and kill the bad practices. No credit crisis has ever disproved that notion any better than the 2007 real estate crash.

The banks were allowed to prescribe whatever they wanted to tens of millions of people. Again, all it means is that you have to seek approval. It's more indirect that you might expect. Like I said earlier, I thought regulating meant that the government told the banks what to lend. It sounded scary and very limiting. People in the industry compare regulation to socialism. These critics feel they'll be handcuffed and watched over 24 hours a day. It reminds of a teenager crying because mom and dad make them call home to report where they are. We need to stop crying about regulation because this is a serious problem.

Those in favor of deregulation will argue that regulating banking will just slow the economy. They will claim that trade will significantly slow and perhaps never reach its real peak. A major flaw in this argument is that the proverbial 'peak' is cosmetic.

The peaks reached after 9/11, for example, is not real. It only took 3-4 years for the whole thing to come falling down. Sure, you can feed an athlete all the steroids and junk available, and they'll peak like a mountain. Two years later, they'll likely crack in half because the body is just not made to endure that stress.

A healthy economy is one that can self-sustain. Recessions will always occur. In fact, recessions are healthy in the overall life of an economy because the recession rids of ineffective trade. However, to just let a few get filthy rich while everybody else suffers is a pretty bad argument. Recently, President Obama suggested limiting all credit card companies' interest rates to a ceiling of 15%. You can just imagine their reaction. Instead of saying 'but we won't make as much money!', they went on the offensive. Creditors claimed they wouldn't be able to offer as much credit and that it would significantly slow the economy. I believe we called their bluff because they don't make much money either by not offering credit! Why would you stop offering credit to people; because you don't get to make as much money on each one? You know what, it sounds like you'd actually have to offer MORE credit to make the same amount!

When you think about it, the government doesn't want anything to do with the actual day to day lending operation. Just like the FDA isn't sitting around coming up with drugs that are available. The pharmaceutical companies are the creative people with the FDA simply acting as mom and dad making sure you won't get hurt. Once a pharmaceutical is approved, it can be prescribed to anybody and everybody.

The whole country was convinced that everything was fine and that the financial sector was healthy. Alan Greenspan was hailed as a genius. He'd come on TV and say everything was perfect. However, those on the top likely knew it would come to a nasty end.

A Doctor prescribing medication at a higher than normal dose is aware of what will happen. The patient, the family, maybe even the pharmacist might not know. However, you have to be ignorant to believe that the individuals on top taking $100 Million didn't know.

In addition to lower credit scores and income, the loan to values changed. You could borrow 80% of the home, and put down 20%. Any individual putting down 20% is a very safe borrower. Whether you have a low or very high credit score, that individual is very unlikely to walk away from a home when he or she puts down 20% of their own money! Not to say that you need to put 20% to be credible. 20% comes out to be lot of money in real estate. I am simply stating that 20% should be a slam-dunk deal for the bank.

I was lending at 90%, 95%, and 100%. Lending at 90 or 95% is not necessarily a dangerous proposition. For the right person, certainly a good majority of people, it's pretty safe. 100% financing is a bit iffy. I feel you should have to invest something of yours to purchase a home. Purchasing a home is a privilege. It's not like buying groceries. Because there is a big responsibility, I feel it is definitely a privilege. Therefore, it should not be made available to any Joe-blow on the street.

Put in the time and you deserve a home. What is the harm of earning your home? I don't want people to take me the wrong way. I believe you should earn your home, but I know damn well that nobody has the right to just take it away either.

This was mostly happening at the subprime level, but also prevalent n the prime market. Working for a major bank started to make me feel like a hitman. Sure, I'd get you the money you needed. However, we're talking 2-3 points and an 11% interest rate. 11% for a secured loan is a bit ridiculous. How much damn money does the bank really need to make? A $500,000 loan at 11% over 30 years earns the bank $1,241,000. Seems a bit steep to me. If you think about it, you're paying $1,741,000 for the home you paid $500,000 for.

Fannie Mae loosened up all the guidelines and EVERYBODY was borrowing. But, you also had Wall Street cleaning up on the sub-prime market. Lehman Brothers, Bear Sterns, etc all got in on the act. The very loose Fannie Mae guidelines I was using was pretty darn liberal. With subprime loans, I could lend to bankrupt borrowers. I once was able to lend $250,000 to a person who had a collection from their local grocery store.

After that, the banks were lending to people one day out of bankruptcy. Bankruptcies stay on credit reports for seven years. When you can longer endure the debt at all and have to throw your arms up in the air, well, that's bankruptcy. I'm glad we live in a country that gives you a second chance, but one day out? Shouldn't you first demonstrate that you could bear something like, say, paying the groceries?

You can see how those thousands of pyramid schemes were spreading viruses to the country. We were all a part of it. None of us wanted to accept the inevitable bubble-burst. We rarely heard about it from economists on TV. It's pretty hard to trust those same idiots that are just selling me their book. If one loan officer stood up and refused to lend because he wanted to wear the white hat….he'd be fired. We were told, if you we didn't do the loan, the guy down the street will.

Everybody loves comparing our economy to the Great Depression. The major difference is that we stepped in immediately and slowed the bleeding quickly. With any deep recession you need to slow the bleeding first which could take quite some time. At that point, the recovery can begin.

In the year 2001, the 2000 recession finally hit America. The collapse of the .com bubble was truly the cause of these recessions, as well as the attacks that occurred on September 11th on the World Trade Center Towers in New York City. Accounting scandals also ran rampant, contributing to the overall downward financial spiral that America faced. Everyone remembers the attacks on America's soil, and nobody will forget how, despite economic trouble, the attacks brought Americans together, more united than ever. And with that kind of perseverance, America was led out of that struggle to a new future of prosperity.

People will ask me, 'but home prices were going up 15%, so it 's ok to lend 100% financing'. With inflation, home prices (cost of a home), will go up like anything else. Real estate is also finite. There is only so much of it. Buy land and you own something limited. The value will go up, of course!

Home prices were not appreciating 15% until AFTER 90-100% financing, loosened guidelines and subprime came along. It's supply and demand! For arguments sake, if 3 out of 10 Americans can qualify for a home loan, the market will be pretty steady. If 6 out of 10 Americans can qualify, the demand goes up unbelievably. 8 out of 10 Americans being able to buy a home because of subprime and loose guidelines will inject steroids into the market. The market was on drugs. You had a finite commodity that was demanded by 3 times the amount of people. The supply was the same for some time, but the demand exploded.

Since the demand exploded onto the scene, homebuilders were implored and enticed to meet that increased demand. If 5 people are fighting for 1 property, why not build 4 more and make a bundle? That is precisely what started happening.

CHAPTER IV

Fallout

We've established how easy it was to borrow money. Nobody was more vulnerable than builders. Keep in mind that we did not anticipate such a turbulent ending.

Home builders benefited from the market in several ways. Banks would lend builders money to build a spec home. Copious speculation homes were built because the demand was there. Banks were being paid off (with their own money!) so they were happy. Think about it. ABC Bank would give the builder money to build the home on speculation. The builder then sold the home to a buyer who went to ABC bank for the mortgage to buy that home. The market was just chasing its tail for years.

Bank downpayments and guidelines are rather precise measurements. Consider how a doctor administers a drug. A pharmaceutical company will experiment carefully, starting very small, observing how the patients respond. Over time the patients will receive a bit more if they were responding well. It takes years and years of medical research to determine what dosage and frequency a medication should be prescribed. The financial guidelines also took years to determine. The guidelines are not just made up out of thin air. It takes some pushing and pulling with very focused analysis of the response. Essentially, after 9/11, in one fell swoop, we threw them all out. The result was a whole country high, wanting more and more.

One way to deceive the bank was to make it appear as if you were going to live in a potential property. If the property was to be 'owner-occupied', you could borrow 100% of the purchase price without hesitation. If they deemed the property to be a vacation home, the bank lent at 90-95%. When a property was being purchased solely for investment purchases, a 15-25% downpayment was pretty typical. These numbers are not arbitrary. It's all about offsetting risk

The Taxpayer Relief Act of 1997 had a significant impact on the financial realities of real property ownership. The act provided taxpayers with substantial tax savings and modified how gains on real property would be taxed. Prior to the passing of the act, a gain on the sale of a primary residence, or principal residence, was taxed at a rate of 28 percent. The new act lowered the rate on capital gains to 20 percent; this rate was further reduced to the current rate of 15 percent on long-term gains.

If a homeowner and his family unfortunately were to run into financial trouble, what is the first thing they will liquidate or sell? Any person will get rid of the property they don't use, don't live in, etc. Therefore, if you are not going to live in the property, the bank will call for a greater down payment. A larger down payment by any borrower will more likely protect the bank from the borrower walking away from the property. In the case that you did walk away from the property, the bank has some wiggle room to work with to recoup their loss. They can sell the property for less than it's worth and likely earn their investment back.

Many builders and homeowners alike were completely abusing this major detail. Builders were telling banks they'd live in the home….and the builder would get 100% financing. It was like robbing the bank. Many builders would use a mortgage broker who could really pull off some tricks. The mortgage broker could go to 10 different banks and close on 10 different properties, all ostensibly owner occupied, at 100% financing. Now, you have a builder with $6 Million in debt. The builder was doing very well. Building a home for $400k and selling it for $600k. Not only was the demand there, but demand was driving appreciation through the roof!

Let's go back to the individuals who were lent money at 95-100%. Those that stated their income, or simply didn't have to state it at all. Perhaps the borrower is only one day out of bankruptcy. It took about a year and a half for this virus to eventually start showing its ugly head. People were refinancing to interest only loans, or negative amortization loans. Then, they couldn't even afford those payments. Late payments began to accrue. Eventually, many had to relinquish the home via foreclosure. When you're hooked on a nasty drug, you can slowly wean off of it. That doesn't work in the world of banking. The repercussions extend much farther into society.

The bubble bursted in late 2007. After foreclosures were becoming more common, everybody from Wall Street to Washington showed their 'uh-oh' face. We immediately pulled back on financing. The guidelines were changing every week because the numbers were reporting the information from the prior month's activity. The market feedback got worse, and worse, and worse. All of a sudden, the banks had to forecast the devastations. They would change guidelines before the reports came out because they knew they'd be worse. The whole trend spiraled downwards.

Typical guidelines could change every month or two, with each variation being announced in advance. By the end of 2007, the guidelines were not changing without any advance notice, but they'd change weekly. When things were at their worst, you'd see three changes in one day.

Gas prices are influenced by supply. The demand is rather stable in comparison to the supply, which could change over night. If a refinery in Texas closes down, the price will change within minutes. Consider a gas station advertising a gallon of 89 octane for $2.49. That morning, news reports that refineries were closed, or a tanker spilled, or perhaps relations with Saudi Arabia were compromised. That gas station would pull the price on that gallon. They would rather be sued than give you the gas for that cheap. The banks were no different.

Fannie Mae would not buy the paper at the guideline a loan was locked in. Let's say a banker locked a loan at 90% loan to value for a 660 credit score. Everything checks out ok. 2 hours later Fannie Mae changes the guideline to a minimum 680 FICO. That means they won't purchase the paper you locked at for the 660 FICO. If they won't buy it, the bank will have to fund and hold the loan using their very own limited vault money, i.e., portfolio money.

In many cases, it would actually cost the bank more to close the loan than renege and be sued! Hypothetically, imagine the bank closes on the loan, then find out they can't sell the paper, therefore forced to hold the loan, that loan defaults…. that bank eventually folds! It was happening by the minute and nobody even had a chance to catch their breath. We were scrambling like Pearl Harbor.

All of a sudden, in no time, the demand drastically slowed in very late 2007. It slowed down too much to the point that people who were well qualified couldn't get a loan. The credit was simply not there. Instead of 4 out of 10 people getting a home, for arguments sake, 2 out of 10 could get a home. Let's imagine what this means for the builder who was building homes thinking 8 out of 10 people could afford a home.

So many builders, whether experienced or new, were increasing that supply to meet the demand. Of course, the builders, like everyone else could not see the dead end coming. Perhaps a slow tapering off of the market was imaginable. However, a completely and utter dead stop is what occurred. The demand fell off the charts because the banks almost stopped lending to the very buyers who intended on purchasing those homes. What transpires is nothing but a cycle of banks stopping their loans to borrowers, less and less people are then buying homes, and the builder who built 5 spec homes is sweating bullets.

Not only were builders owning 5 properties, but they were likely expensive. People were purchasing $400,000-$800,000 homes so easily. The country was on a spending frenzy. Borrowers, who could really only qualify for $300k, were being lent $700k. Remember the debt ratios? It was once 36%, then it shot up to numbers even in the 70%'s. How about the stated income guy who stated twice what he really made. People spent like it was going out of style. Americans suffered and the builders really suffered. Unlike the average American who simply couldn't afford the one home they owned, builders couldn't afford the 5 homes they owned!

I know of builders who were paying up to $100,000 a month in mortgage payments (including taxes and insurance). What they were doing was just leveraging the banks money against the home. Builders were investing almost none of their own money and walking away with 6-7 figure profits. It was the smart thing to do. The not-so-smart thing to do was build 4, 5, or 10 homes at the same time.

Time and time again, a builder borrowed $400k, paid the bank off and walked away with $100k. Sounds like a dream job! However, to borrow 100% financing and stated income, the loan would have to close subprime, which meant a 10% rate. Still, they built it, and usually sold the project before it was even finished! After 2, 5, 10, 30, or 60 successful sales, anybody would start getting risky, especially if the bank was throwing them the money to build.

When the market crashed it wasn't fun anymore. The builder maybe sold a home or two, but he was holding onto that home for longer. That's not a terrible proposition if you're selling 1 or 2 at a time. However, if we're talking 4 or 5 mansions, which nobody can afford to buy anymore, it was just a matter of time. Perhaps he borrowed more and more bad and expensive debt to help pay those mortgages. Most builders just felt it would turn around rather quickly. They thought they just needed to weather the storm. The end never came and they just led to a slow credit death. If the builder was big enough, he may have even been lucky enough to make the local newspaper. Eventually, the banks took over the homes through foreclosure. The builder was left with nothing, but demolished credit, bankruptcy filings, or lawsuits. Many have tax liens or restitution to pay.

Don't get the impression that all builders are out of business. That is hardly the case. If it were, you'd see some very ugly pictures on TV that would really resemble the Great Depression. However, there are more cases than there should be. That's where you come in.

CHAPTER V

The Turnaround

You might be asking yourself, 'what good can come out of all this?' It is natural to feel tentative and wonder if we will ever recover. It's not a matter of if we will recover, but when? Our market was wired to operate like a see-saw. Anything that goes up must come down, and anything that goes down must come up. The market is a cycle of feeding and ridding itself,.

The most simplistic account of a recession is 'an imbalance between supply and demand'. Sounds a little like a see-saw, doesn't it? Well, it has been and always will. However, it's time to revisit the seeds that companies purchase and harbor until they grow. This chapter will illustrate how you will take advantage of the turmoil.

Cheer up! The good news is that it will all turn out for the good. People were buying plenty of homes before this whole mess happened. In fact, the current 2007+ recession is a blip on the radar in the history of home ownership!

Builders in every town and city have gone out of business. They can't work because they lost their credit or lost their license because of tax liens. However, these builders are still very excellent entrepreneurs and tradesmen. Remember, builders did not go out of business because they made a poor product. These builders simply did not balance their expenses or they completely overleveraged their work. This recession will go down as one of the biggest economic tidal waves to hit the world. It set up so many people for failure. Hundreds upon thousands of banks, domestic, and global were infected with this recession bug.

Detroit auto manufacturer failures are the definition of companies going bankrupt because of a bad product. The cars were overpriced and under-performing compared to the competition. The 2007 recession simply exposed them just like it exposed other companies, such as Circuit City. The credit crisis burned them in the long-run, but consider all the other brands that survived.

Contractors and builders were doing very well before lending guidelines loosened. In the early 2000's, builders were living well. Same as in the 1990's, the 1980's, etc. We have had more builders and subcontractors enter the market since the 1980's than pre-Reagan. Even the evolution of Home Depot in the early 1980's was a key contributor to making remodeling a household term, no pun intended. In their first 20 years, Home Depot grew more than any other retail outfit, including Wal-Mart. Before Home Depot, homeowners were relegated to local mom and pop shops or mediocre retail stores with no customer service.

We discussed how 2002-2007 prompted an explosion in the economic climate. Review the history of the Dow Jones Industrial Average and you'll realize to what extent, On October 19, 1987, the Dow plunged 507 points, which will always be remembered as the Black Monday Crash. 507 points might not seem a lot today, but in 1987, the Dow closed at 1,738 points! The Dow didn't exceed 6,000 points until only October 14, 1996.

From October, 1997's 6,000 point average to January 2000, the Dow shot up to 11,500. That comes to 5,500 points in a little over 2 years. The tech boom of the late 1990's is almost laughable in comparison to the entire Dow Jones history. Between 1896 and 1989, a history of almost 100 years, the Dow totaled a 2,100 point increase.

After 9/11 the Dow Jones 'plunged' to 7,286 by October 2002. However, the beginning-middle of 2003 is when the see-saw tilted once again. The United States and most of the other first rate global economies experienced almost 4 straight years of nothing but gain after gain. July 2007 brought us our first close above 14,000. You already know what happened next; the recession of 2007. Once again, we slid back down. On March 9, 2009 the Dow Jones closed at 6,547.05. The country thought it would never stop. I believe some thought it would drop down to 0! And in only 7 months, it literally skyrocketed to over 10,000 points on October 14, 2009.

Doesn't this all sound familiar by now? Are you getting tired of hearing about how the 2007 recession is just another piece of the history pie? Somehow, an average of 10,000 is just scary to the media. I think they've lost perspective, yet again. Have you watched a see-saw lately? Has it changed? When one side hits the bottom do you really freak out? Of course, it goes up in a matter of seconds. The market can't go back up in a matter of seconds, so let's just all grow up. In the early 1930's, when the Great Depression had carried on for a few years, John D. Rockefeller said that "These are days when many are discouraged. In the 93 years of my life, depressions have come and gone. Prosperity has always returned and will again." How right he was, more often than he'd like to know.

We've established the fact that the recession of 2007 was inevitable and unavoidable. However, every builder or tradesmen I have met is incredibly humble from the experience. If people were not purchasing homes in 2010, I can understand builders being concerned; how couldn't they be? I promise you that the construction tradesmen are not scared. They might be struggling, but they know their skills will always be needed! Their attitude is almost 'when you people in Washington finally figure this out and fix it, we'll be here waiting'. These builders are now better at what they do because of it. I bet GM will produce an incredibly better car after filing bankruptcy.

The world is becoming more efficient. Everything is more 'green', environmentally friendly, and less wasteful. You can bet that builders will be constructing more efficient homes. We're not going to be building as many mini-mansions or $500k+ valued homes. Too many people who belong in a $350k home were getting approved for the $475k or $600k house. Here's a crazy thought: put people in homes that they can really afford.

Consider the wealth that builders were bringing in before everything collapsed. Mind you, it will never be quite the frenzy, but things will become very active again. They already have! And it will continue to grow better and healthier because banks won't otherwise thrive. Remember, this country is built on banks and small business lending. The banks simply need to be monitored a bit more. After this piece of history is over, banks will loosen the slack again, but this time around, they'll know when to tie off the rope. It's already happening and it will expand.

Just like prescribing medication, we will return to a safe level of lending. The United States as a whole went overboard and now the response was under-lending. Banks were under-prescribing and the economy naturally slowed from it. You can bet that everything will return to stability, which is really when the big bucks will roll in.

The point of this manual is to take the positives out of this opportunity. Most people go into hiding because of their perception of all the contradicting information they're barraged with. I am attempting to make the information simple for you.

The main reason people will naturally rescind or virtually cease all investment activity is because of the unknown factor. The public, in general, does not understand the dilemma. Driving a car can be dangerous; people have lost their lives. However, every time something bad happened in a car, it was followed with a detailed explanation. Same thing with airplane crashes. If people died in cars, and an investigation leading to the reason why was never presented, EVERYBODY would be afraid to drive. However, we all understand what the dangerous parts are. The more superior understanding you have of any situation, the more successfully you will negotiate it.

You'll find an 'expert' every other day on TV giving their opinion about the current state of the economy. One day we're doomed, the next it's all peaches and cream. Like you, I'm tired of all the contrasting beliefs and advice given every single day. It's like making a final decision on a player's performance halfway through the basketball game. Let the game finish and then make your report. In fact, you'll find reporters crucify a player one day after a bad performance and then be in love with him a week later. Have we lost our ability to be patient?

Economists are very intelligent and well-informed people. These are people with advanced degrees, years of experience, and connections to some of the most powerful people. Trust me, economists and financial analysts don't get their information from cable news shows and neither should you. When they step onto a TV set and make predictions like Jimmy 'The Greek' Snyder, you just need to take it for what it is. Whether it's CBS Sports or CNN, it's still all TV. Trust your instinct a lot more than television news reports

Most of the time, we look to the media to inform us of the current state of the affairs; not exactly a wild idea. We've relied on media for current affairs since the printing press was invented. However, it's almost impossible to find a media source that truly is bi-partisan. Heads of networks, for example, are lobbied. If you enjoy watching CNN or Fox, that's great. However, CNN is owned by Ted Turner, a dedicated Democrat. Therefore, even your 'news' is biased. Of course, you can't create news, but you can certainly present it differently. If the US President is a Democrat, the Republican biased networks will invite more critics of his onto their sets. Maybe what the President is doing is fantastic, but you just watched some 'expert' tear him a new one.

News shows are broadcasted 24 hours a day. You might have enough national news to fill a few hours each day. The rest is opinion, critics, debates, etc. If you have 15 news shows on, they are all competing for your ratings. That means it becomes a business of entertainment. If it were just news, each network should have the same ratings. It'll never happen because we are all partisan. Some advertisers might care, some won't. Again, every company on this planet is run by executives who have a political predisposition. In some cases, you'll have companies like the automotive industry, alcohol, or tobacco, who lobby the hell out of politicians. If a company receives Republican political support, you think they'll advertise on a Democratic-oriented network? This isn't a whole conspiracy theory. Your brain won't be warped, nor will you turn into a robot if you watch too much of it. Ultimately, so many people incorporate what they see on TV into their daily lives. So, the overall point is : rely on your own opinion and instincts a lot more because they don't come with nearly the agenda.

We cannot compare today's activity to the post 9/11 boom. The whole country was on drugs spending and borrowing like there was no tomorrow. Today's market is not terrible. It is certainly tougher, but it could be so much worse. Remember when a few baseball players were hitting 70 homeruns a season? Those statistics were likely influenced by performance enhancing drugs. However, these days, if a player hits 40 homeruns in a season we now consider that average. Are you kidding? That's a lot of homeruns when you gain a perspective and history of the game. For heavens sake, just because you can't borrow $2mm from the bank doesn't mean we're screwed.

According the National Association of Realtors, existing home sales peaked at over 7.2 million units in 2005. In 2006 saw a small decline of 6,478,000 existing home sales. The market declined in 2007 to 5,652,000 and further in 2008 to 4,913,000. 2009 is on the upswing bringing us back to 2007 numbers. According to all the 'experts' and millions of news blogs, the country is in a near depression. A recent news clip actually made the case that you can look to trends in pop-culture to help explain the swings in the financial market. I don't know what comparison these people will come up with next, but I won't be reading that one either.

While we're on the subject of the Great Depression, let's quickly review what was a 10+ year history of economic disorder. Unlike the 2007 recession, the rich and poor experienced devastating consequences. Unemployment was over 30% in some parts of the world and you can forget about construction. There was practically no real estate building.

Even 70 years after the Great Depression, there are varying opinions as to what caused the infamous crash. However, consider what would happen if the Great Depression occurred today. Our world is so connected (perhaps too connected) in comparison to the 1930's. If a small bank in a zip code in California was to fail, an investment firm in Bangkok would know about it 10 minutes later. Today, we'd identify the issue so much quicker. Instead of 10+ years, perhaps we'd resolve the global crisis in 3 years. Hmm, does this sound familiar? Let's continue.

2008 was one of the most tumultuous financial years in the entire history of United States economy. Banks were closing in every city. Lehman Brothers and Bear Sterns weren't immune to this plague. Even still, close to 5 million real estate units sold in 2008. I may not have the most optimistic, cheerleader personality, but are those numbers really that atrocious? Remember, we can't compare home sales to 2005, or 2006. First of all, those statistics were all delivered with the help of 'performance enhancing lending'. Second, we'll never hit those numbers.

What goes up must come down in our market. The higher the market peaks, the harder the crash we'll be. In order to be healthy, we need a happy medium. Of course, Capitalism doesn't run parallel with the 'happy medium' very well. Besides, the 2009 home sales statistics are pretty darn decent. Just imagine what they'll be when we actually hit our stride again.

The reason why it's difficult to analyze the market is because it's not an exact science. There have been dozens of recessions, tougher credit or bear markets in the 20th century. And they all pretty much happened for different reasons. It's not like the banks arbitrarily just stop lending or lose money. An investment comes to fruition, it's overleveraged, and then the banks suffer.

Comparing today's market to other times is like comparing apples to oranges. It really is. Imagine the early 1980's being a pear, late 80's a peach, early to mid 1990's a banana, late 1990's boom to an orange, tech boom of early 2000's a strawberry, post 9/11 boom an apple, and the 2007 recession a kiwi. They all might be fruit, but they're the farthest thing from being the same. The country's recessions or bear markets might all seem the same to the public because one day money is available, and the next it isn't. However, all of the booms and crisis were as unique as fruit! They were spurred by different situations.

Even the video game era of the early 1980's had a boom and crash. Atari's Pong and Atari 2600 were huge hits. Naturally, they stimulated competition which therefore created a 'market'. Atari's home Pong system exploded only after Sears helped make it popular. Nintendo was originally a playing cards company. Their first hit was Donkey Kong, which needless to say, blasted off everywhere, along with their video game console. However, after Warner Bros. purchased Atari, they started running it like a strict corporation and it eventually folded. The crash of Atari brought the video game market to it's knees and almost destroyed it. Head game programmers from Atari and Apple left to start independent companies such as EA.

A Japanese engineer was taking his staff to lunch where they shared a pizza pie. After somebody took the first slice out of the pie the engineer couldn't sit still. Pacman was born. The video game world lived on with the help of Nintendo. Booms and crashes have happened because of every damn innovation and it will continue to do so.

The point is that this recession or credit crisis is nothing new. It was been born and reborn so many times. Capitalism is heavily driven by shareholders. What do shareholders want ...profit. Corporations' sole purpose is to make money. Forget the environment or anything else that comes in its way. Once Liz Claiborne was incorporated, she lost control of the company to a board of lawyers, accountants and investors. But, guess what ...companies cannot turn profits forever; it's impossible! It's absolutely naïve to think that a company can continue to grow infinitely. Wall Street and all its shareholders will run a boom dry until it crashes, and then move onto another. THAT'S how Wall Street thinks it can make profits forever.

The 1980's brought a real boom to the stock market, which evidently still exists today. Average Joes buy stock in companies like they're investing or betting on a racehorse. Any human who can operate a telephone and a checkbook can buy stock. You don't need to know what the heck the company does. You certainly don't have to be familiar with employees, CEO, structure, financial plan, investment strategy; you know, the nuts and bolts of a company. Somebody with enough money can own 5% and not know if the company makes shoes or condoms.

If a trainer knows he has 10 million people betting on his horse, what do you think he will do? He will scratch and claw and likely cheat. The horse is whipped, it wins, and it's whipped even more and more. The stock grows, more people bet on it, the pressure is added. The problem is, like a horse, you can't just whip it forever. No company can grow forever. For one, we create anti-trust laws so no company can monopolize a system. Therefore, on one hand, we want a fair market place, and on the other, we have shareholders who want more, more, more return. The company quickly loses its vision. Eventually, corners may be cut and even greater than normal risks are taken. Once it's overleveraged in poor investments, it crashes. The 10 Million average Joe's who don't know a lick scream for their money back. They blame the system. Everybody wants justice. Welcome to the recession.

Now, a reason the current recession is so grave is because it includes real estate which goes hand in hand with bank credit. Unlike video games, the tentacles of real estate failure extends so deep and far into every nook and cranny of the market.

When I hear some 'expert' analyzing our economy or comparing it to others, I turn the channel. It's not easy to analyze the market. It's so complex that the most advanced computers can't predict outcomes. In most cases, we learn after the fact about what happened.

It's not the recession that is scaring the public. It is the lack of understanding! Earlier, I explained how the rich get richer because of their willingness to collect the immensely discounted seeds during times like these. Sure, many individuals who have the money to lose can prosper and survive. However, the majority of people who clean up don't have billions or millions in their bank account. The common denominator is an investor's understanding of what is occurring.

When I helped start a building company, I was in debt. It all happened from one bad real estate transaction, but I also had monies invested in some property. The reason I purchased real estate was because it was so cheap. I didn't have a million dollars to start with! However, I was in the easiest race I could imagine. 75% of the contestants backed out on their own and went into hiding. Everybody was so timid. It's a dream come true. No waiting in line to make money!

I'm telling you that if you pass on this opportunity you'll be kicking yourself. Don't be a statistic for heavens sake. If a major department store was selling all their merchandise 70% off, people would come running! But, when it comes to purchasing homes cheap they hide in their closets. HUH??!!!! You'll spend money on discounted clothes, but you won't purchase discounted real estate and make 6 figures? Am I missing something here?

What we're missing is the information. It's the media and general fear that is being instilled. The internet, blogs, 20 cable news channels; it's everywhere! And people can't tell heads from tails anymore.

However, what do rich and successful people have in spite of all the noise broadcasted along the internet and TV? They have **perspective**. These people are not caught up in the drama like it's a soap opera. Just look at our country's history, some trends, etc. This recession will end and you can bet every damn nickel on it. The market will get back on it's feet and start running like a track star again. You can be right there with it. The track star will get tired and have to rest. You'll be there for that, and you'll know that it will all start over again, and again, and again.

The best investors don't live for today. They live for tomorrow, the weeks after, and years after. They play the numbers! It's perspective. The people with perspective to purchase those seeds are going to clean up. Get off your butt and take your own stake. Otherwise, somebody else will.

Q and A's:

1. <u>Why can't builders just get their own credit?</u>

A collection account on a credit report can drop a score significantly. A judgment is even worse. Moreover, after the 2007 recession, a bankruptcy is the deal breaker. Such derogatory accounts remain on a credit report for up to 7 years.

FICO calculations have also tightened up recently. You need better performance on your accounts to score higher. There are builders who believe they will never get their credit back. For the time being, FICO is set up to make it almost impossible for these individuals to recover. I do not believe that FICO is the best system, but it is a very difficult system to change.

Unfortunately, for the builder, it will be quite some time before they can get their credit back to where it once was. Credit is like a pool of water. You must keep it clean and flowing. If you let a drop of oil fall in, it will spread everywhere. The only way to get rid of the oil is to slowly filter out the whole pool with clean water. You can't just remove the water and put fresh water in there. That's how FICO credit works. Bad debt must slowly be replaced with clean, new debt. And after that, the clean new debt must be maintained for it to even be worth anything!

2. <u>If a builder failed before, isn't it proof that he will fail again?!</u>

Consider why the builder you are working with failed. If they never were doing well before, then find another business partner. The right business partner is essential, but, you just need to find one. This isn't like putting together a restaurant menu. One solid, established builder is all that is needed.

There are tons of builders that were thriving. There are millions of small business owners that have nothing to do with real estate who had to fold as well. The recession really cleaned many business owners out. However, instead of just a random small business, we are talking about real estate. Real Estate and new construction MUST thrive in this country. It is a barometer of every economy.

Another thought is that real estate will never really change. It's not like people will start living in hammocks. Many small businesses or innovations do have a half-life. They have to really stay on their toes and grow with the world. However, my plan concentrates on the most basic necessity that requires little to no start up Capital.

Every boom such as video games or .com ended up passing because of an evolution in the market. Perhaps a better product is made available, or we just no longer rely on the technology. Real estate, on the other hand, might be the most linear necessity of all. It always has been profitable and always will be.

Unlike stocks, land is finite. A company that makes sneakers, for example, can be replaced over and over and over again. You can't make any more land. For the last 4 billion years and the next 4 billion years, we know exactly how much land there was and will be. Not only does it make it a great investment, it makes it the most stable investment. We can see billions of years into the future and know precisely what the supply will be. Can you say that about any other industry? Even gold, diamonds or silicone is robust. Commodities are incredibly more stable than the stock market, however, the supply is still not fixed. It takes the earth awfully long to create a diamond, however, we do know that as we speak, the earth is churning out commodities. If the earth could create more real estate, wow what a different scenario it would be. But, it's not.

3. <u>You say a recession is cyclical. So does this mean this is all just going to happen again? Why would I invest if it will fail again?</u>

Recessions are cyclical. However, we have learned from every single one of them. Not only will lending be more efficient, so will home building. We will not be running into the same mistakes. The .com recession taught us a lot about the internet and web-based companies. Since then , it has cleaned up because we learned the hard way.

It is difficult to accept the fact that the best way to avoid a disaster is by learning from witnessing it in the first place. Unlike many scenarios, we couldn't just experiment in a lab, a practice field, or a computer simulation. We had to watch it unfold in front of our eyes. However, now we know what we've done wrong.

Imagine a doctor or a lawyer that has spent their whole life learning their trade, perfecting it. They are committed to what they do 100%. Contractors are very similar. Mortgage brokers, bankers, and realtors are all revolving-door industries. People come and go so often with the true players who stick around. However, contractors had to spend an immense amount of time and training to get to where they were. It is a real shame that they had to unfold. Not only do they have the knowledge, but they also have the right contacts, which we will discuss later.

Another recession will occur. You can expect to experience several in your lifetime. However, it's nothing but an opportunity to herd more seeds into your collection.

The difference between a Warren Buffet and a failed builder was their preparation. Recessions are a time for buying, not selling. The failed builders just couldn't endure the period of time. They tried to continue to sell, but it was all at the worst time. If the failed builder had more reserves, and could invest during the recession, he'd come out the other end of the recession richer. When the next recession came along, the builder would invest again, and again, come out even richer than before.

The failed builder blew his/her whole wad at once.. To his credit, nobody expected the tide to stop dead in it's tracks. The demand was so artificial and we will likely never see it again.

4. <u>Banks have tightened tremendously. How far will they really loosen up again?</u>

Banks function just like the revolving door or any retail market. Merchandise gets loaded through the back door and sold out the front door. For example, a grocery store stocks steaks, chicken, etc in their freezer. As customers purchase their product, they order more. When the bank writes a loan for a borrower, they sell the product out the back door. It's basically the same principle because instead of steaks, banks' have their own product. It's called paper.

Banks lend and sell loans not just to investors but also between one another. In any healthy market, there is a consistent flow of merchandise (paper). Just like the spin of the earth, which also contributes to the movement of the water in the oceans and the air in the skies. Day after day, it really does feed into and off itself.

Obviously, the more reliable the paper, the better the product. The better the product, the more of it they can sell. When mortgage defaults were popping up all over the place, investors pulled their money out of mortgage paper and put it into something else. When banks can no longer bring in investors to purchase the loans they write, lending comes to a halt.

A grocery store could re-stock their shelves any time and at any rate. However, what would happen if they could no longer re-order their steaks and chicken for the freezer? Imagine what would happen to their current supply. Not only would it be more expensive, but the grocery store would be extra careful who they'd sell it to.

When banks couldn't sell their paper so easily, boy did they pull back on the guidelines big time. They overcompensated by making it extra difficult to get a loan. In the case they did write a loan, it was most likely a great product because they did their extra due diligence. This is why banks went from handing out loans to anybody to all of a sudden practically asking for blood and urine samples. They want to make sure that if they give you this money, you won't screw it up. The more paper they write which doesn't default, the more confidence the banking industry gains with investors. People who should get loans were still denied because the banks had no choice. The amount of steaks were so finite they didn't care who the heck you were or how much money you had. Everybody now had to wait on the same line, whether they were putting 40% down or 3.5% down.

Yes, it was unfair for some time, but the banks had no choice and we really need to appreciate the dilemma they were in. The great news is that we are sure all the loans the banks are lending will be safe. Plenty of people still have bad loans or are underwater, which is still fallout from the boom-times.

When the market started crashing in late 2007, we were most likely seeing defaults from loans lent several years earlier. Investors over panicked because if 2007 was exposing the defaults from several years earlier, imagine what we're up for when all the 2006 and 2007 loans start defaulting. It will just add to the heap of bad debt. Put yourself in their shoes. It wasn't like a bad sports bet. We're talking about a bad global bet which had trillions of dollars on the line!!

Similar to personal credit, we need to filter out bad debt with good debt. It takes time, but it will always come out clean on the other end. Sometimes it could take 9 months, or longer. People want to pay their mortgage. They just don't pay their mortgage when they simply can't.

The guidelines for conforming and nonconforming loans will eventually loosen a bit, step by step. It's all about testing the market. When they're ready, you'll notice minimum credit scores going down a bit. However, the banks then have to gauge the market's response. Just like administering a higher dose of a drug to test patients, you first over-analyze how they respond to it. When the banks are positive that the market is responding well to loosened guidelines they loosen them again.

The non-conforming market is not government backed like a Fannie Mae or Freddie Mac. Rather, it is filled with portfolio loans or those purchased by private investors. Those too will eventually become immunized and therefore be able to take on more risk.

The market crash was similar to an ER patient being rushed into the hospital. First, you stabilize the patient, after which he or she is immediately prepped for any necessary operation. After that, it's a slow recovery. Eventually, you introduce solid foods and more stimuli, right? When the patient goes home, he's still monitored and restricted. That slowly phases out. Ultimately, after careful observation and doctor approval, the patient is out playing tennis again!

CHAPTER VI

Business Model

THE CHAPTER YOU'VE BEEN WAITING FOR

We've covered, in great detail, a history of the US economy and the place recessions have within. Moreover, you should now understand why not only the real estate industry took a recent hit, but how many builders were completely overwhelmed.

In order to help make sense of how Wealth Innovative works, I have split up the chapter into two sections. Part A will give you an awesome idea of a construction project's process. Always keep in mind that your job is not to learn how to build. That's your builder's job.

Part B will break down the Wealth Innovative timetable, and explain the 3 simple steps in great detail. You won't believe how simple it is, but I'd rather over simplify it then take anything for granted.

A

Builder 101

Ok, let's get to work. I will now outline exactly what is needed, and illustrate how quickly this will work for you. It's time to talk about the fun stuff. You can probably guess that the purpose of the plan is to start a building company. What you don't know is how easy it is. Let's review how a building company works.

In order to operate effectively, a builder typically has a dozen accounts set up with various vendors for specific materials. Every construction company will need accounts that include, but not limited to, the following services:

- General Materials (Home Depot)
- Lumber/Millwork/Cabinetry
- Roofing and Windows
- Siding
- Paint
- Custom Interior Design
- Container Service (Dumpsters)
- Carpet
- Appliances
- Drywall

There are several vendors that a builder could have access to. Perhaps one has better pricing on trusses, while another may simply offer a better deal on studs. In many situations, you'll find a national chain for each and every account.

With every transaction there are a small handful of consistent necessities. A General Contractor is an intermediary between the vendors and his trade/labor. Similar to car customizing shops, the GC's job is to make sure the clients, the design, and the materials are on hand.

Below is a simple rendering of how the average GC is setup. It is not very complicated:

TABLE A

| Subcontractor | Subcontractor | Subcontractor | Subcontractor | Subcontractor |

Licensed Contractor

| Roofing | Siding | Interior-design | Appliances | Dumpster | General-materials | Paint | Lumber/Milwork |

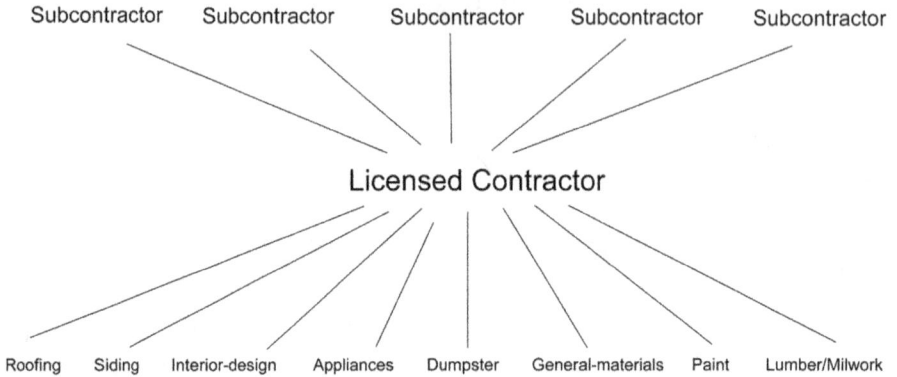

I'll first take you through your garden-variety builder transaction. The terms Builder and General Contractor (GC) will be used interchangeably, however they refer to the same person.

λ The contractor will advertise in a home magazine, postcards, perhaps TV. In many cases, realtors or past clients will be referring business to the contractor anyway. You'll be hearing plenty of people say 'nice to see _____ going again." Anyway, when Client Z is ready, he/she/they calls Builder A to discuss some potential renovation or build.

λ When Builder A meets with Client Z, the two discuss, plan and design what type of remodel or new home build the client would like and what their budget is. In his/her own time, Builder A draws the plans for the project and estimates the job with a cost breakdown. The builder will also meet with several subcontractors to help estimate and get 'bids' for the project. Depending on the complexity of the job, Builder A might be able to get this done himself.

The more experienced builder will be able to accurately estimate the costs, most often, without having to do much work. A truly talented builder has had so much experience, they can really get it down to +/- 1 or 2% of the costs, like a good mechanic who can at least give you an idea of what you're really looking at. They've just done it hundreds of times. However, they still need a real accurate invoice from the vendor because, obviously, prices generally fluctuate.

To reiterate, a banker really relies on guidelines handed down by the bank and Fannie Mae. A builder is an artistic, skilled tradesman. These people are gifted and often sell their clients on their personal touch. It is their personal pride, and important that you do not interfere with their work. After all, why would you want to?

λ Client Z loves Builder A's plan and price. Builder A asks Client Z to sign a Builder Contract and place a downpayment of approximately $10,000. The Builder already has all of this documentation prepared and it's at his discretion. The downpayment is used to secure a building permit and to really make sure the client doesn't walk away. After all, the builder is really working for free until the project begins.

Similar to any regular job,. a builder will receive periodic draws from a bank once work is done. If you just start a new job, your first paycheck won't come for 2-3 weeks, right? Well, for the initial materials and labor, the builder really needs some earnest money to go along with the contract. A building permit can be several thousand dollars just in itself. This is also why a builder simply cannot work without credit. Since most materials and labor is only paid for AFTER, the builder needs to order all the lumber, trusses, sub-flooring, etc on credit.

λ Client Z might have an equity line of credit, or perhaps the moneys is kept in escrow at the title company. In most cases, Builder A begins work on the project. The Builder begins ordering all the necessary materials that are needed and make sure subcontractors and labor is prepared.

Often times, Builder A will work on the project for the first phase or two to make sure everything goes well. After all, a mistake made early on is so much more damaging than a minor detail that can be fixed later.

λ It could be a few weeks, but the builder will request a draw to pay the labor that worked on the project up until that time. Like any trade, work is done, followed by paying that person. Just like as if you had a plumber come to your home. You don't pay upfront. The work is done first.

Not only will the GC pay the labor partially, but the GC ordered most of the materials on credit. The roof, Home Depot, windows materials guys all need to be paid. The GC usually has a credit limit depending on the vendor. He will almost max that limit, then pay it down, and do it again. If Builder A doesn't pay it down on Client Z's invoice, not only will work be suspended on Client Z' project, but perhaps the other 5 client's he signed will also be delayed. It is 100% imperative that the GC manage those books efficiently.

There is no reason why these accounts can't be paid. Here is the reason why: A GC will not order one nail unless that nail is needed. No materials are ordered, unless you have a signed Builder Contract and the project is ready to go. The GC doesn't keep stock of materials like a mechanic. He plans/designs, then sends that list to the vendor. It is actually quite simple.

Remember, Builder A has done this numerous times. Don't bombard yourself with the details on the micro-level. I am simply laying this out for your own knowledge so you can at least follow along with the process. After experiencing it on your own once or twice, it will be all second nature to you anyway.

Like knowing the rules to baseball, basketball, etc. All I'm doing is putting the basic rules down so you can follow the game. And, yes, it's ok to be the spectator here too!

λ. A typical project will have several 'draws'. A draw is just like a withdrawal of money after work is done. Again, work is done, money is 'drawn' to pay for that work done. It's a 1:1 ratio. Never do you draw more money than is needed to pay for whatever work is done, nor underdraw.

With every draw, the GC keeps a partial commission for himself. Just about every GC pays him/herself throughout the process. It's not one lump sum just at the end. These fees can range from 10-25% of the cost of the project. It depends on the contract, the complexity of the job, etc. However, GC can be paid very handsomely and they certainly deserve their commission.

λ Once a project is complete, all subcontractors sign a lien waiver, which illustrates that they have been paid in full. With a signed lien waiver, nobody is liable for any money. Again, the GC is familiar with this document. Just like getting a receipt after you pay that plumber who came over. You don't want any gray areas or questions marks later on. The lien waivers will be collected and submitted to the bank or title company so you can then get the next draw. When we were young, mom probably didn't let us reload our plate until we first eat everything up on the first one we had.

By the end of the project, all the materials have been paid for. Not $1 should come out of the GC's pocket, unless there was an unforeseeable issue or mistake. Everybody is otherwise happy and the GC moves onto Client X. Any good GC can maintain 10 projects at the same time. Everything should be planned, well beforehand.

In essence, each project is like its own little short lived company. The small business operates efficiently with the hiring of a manager who oversees the employees and day to day operations. With a build or remodeling contract, the general contractor's duty is similar to that of the store manager. He puts the plan together, then hires subcontractors (like employees) to carry it out some work. The GC manages the project. Most General Contractors will outsource subcontractors such as plumbers, framers, electricians, HVAC, excavators, concrete foundation. Hence, the term General Contractor. The General Contractor is familiar with all the trades, but might not be licensed in a specific arena. The GC's role is to really see the big picture and bring it all together.

In any event, the GC will need the aforementioned accounts set up. First of all, in many cases, you cannot deal direct with these vendors without an account. Secondly, the GC will get a better deal on materials with such an account.

Another purpose for the account is for client services. With many remodels, the GC will send Client Z to ABC Carpet, ABC Appliance store, ABC Interior-Design. The client has a budget, and selects the specific items on their own agenda. Everything is placed and organized neatly under that GC account.

The GC will have a list of subcontractors that he/she uses on a regular basis. With experience, and reputation the GC simply has earned a rapport with subs. You will likely not really deal with subcontractors. If you do, it is pretty rare and it'll likely be to deliver checks (the fun part). There is just a respect that is well deserved and earned when working together on job sites. Moreover, any sub that can expect repeated work from a GC will obviously deliver his most competitive pricing. Most subcontractors are paid directly by the GC twice monthly. The GC usually has a predetermined scheduled that is agreed upon. This way, the GC is not getting calls everyday to cut checks. The check is delivered and in return you bring the lien waiver back to the office.

To reiterate, the GC will pay the invoices for the materials as they come in. It is imperative that you understand how important credit is to a GC. It is the foundation and assembly line of the company. The GC's credit with those vendors is crucial. In many instances, a GC will have more than one project going on. If he/she is not current with a vendor, they can temporarily shut down the account and all of the GC's projects come to a halt. If the GC doesn't pay the invoice for Job A, the clients of Job B are now going to face a delay. The GC will earn a horrible reputation.

The last situation you want to be in is to have a 2nd project running and then stop dead in its tracks. For example, you don't cut a check for the lumber on the first deal, the mill denies a load for the 2nd job site. Now, you look pretty pathetic to client #2. Their home or remodel is being delayed because of an accounting error on your part.

Trust me; every client monitors their job like a baby. They'll drive by the site twice a day just to watch work being done on it. If a tornado comes through town, they might still expect you to be out there working. The point is, a day or two of work stoppage is a very bad thing. Especially if work is stopped because a vendor won't deliver material due to a past due bill.

λ A project could take 4 weeks or 4 months. When it's done, the job is complete and the GC is paid in full. Client Z and Builder A are happy with each other, shake hands, and move on with their respective lives. There is no celebration or party.

There will be a case, however, when the client does not pay the GC in full. Perhaps the client doesn't feel that the work wasn't up to par or complete. On the other hand, a client might just, unfortunately, not have the money anymore. In any event, the GC will immediately place a mechanic's lien on the property.

The mechanic's lien will be recorded, with the rest of the open liens, at the local courthouse. When the owner tries to refinance, sell, or change ownership in anyway, they will not be able to successfully do so. The Mechanic's Lien will ensure that the builder is paid before anybody else gets their share.

If the owner of the property sells the home, the buyer cannot take ownership until the mechanics liens are paid. The buyer simply won't receive clean title to the property. We're not talking about a box of popcorn. A home is the most expensive investment for just about every human being and nobody will assume ownership of a home with liens against it.

In order to transfer the title, the mechanics liens (as well as any other liens) must be paid. Same is true with property tax liens. If you have a property tax lien on your property, you better not make any plans until they're paid.

B

Wealth Innovative Business Model

Always keep in mind that your job is simply to provide the builder with the materials to begin working again.

You don't have to sustain the company, but rather get its engine re-started. The train was already built, working, and on it's track. I'll illustrate how that train was built and what makes it tick, for your own information.

In the coming pages, I will explain the following elements required to start your business:

1. Contractors License

2. Find your Builder

3. Choose Business name

4. Acquire Insurance

5. Obtain a Business License

6. Attain LLC and TIN under business name

7. Business Checking Account

8. Set-up Vendors

9. Open the doors to business!!

Now that we established how a builder takes a project from A to Z, we can dive into how the operation.

Wealth Innovative Timetable
easy as 1-2-3!

1. Business License

Day 1-6

a. Contractor's License
- A contractor's license is very simply to acquire! As easy as completing a short online class, and passing an online open book exam!
We will discuss this in detal later.

Day 6-30

b. Find your Buillder
- So many ways to discover your builder, which is thoroughly explained in the coming pages. Keep in mind you only need 1 !
We will discuss this in detal later.

Day 30-40

c. Acquire Insurance License
- About as easy as getting car insurance. All you need is the state minimum requirements.
We will discuss this in detal later.

2. Business Checking Account

Day 36-38

a. LLC
- Can be filed electronically, overnight. All that's needed is a unique name and abusiness address
We will discuss this in detail later.

Day 38-40

b. TIN
- Tax Payer Identification number is required for any business. It's like a social security number for your business. Without it, you cannot setup most accounts, including a checking account
We wil discuss this in detal later.

3. Building Vendors

Day 40-60

- Very minimum credit & a few references (provided by your builder) is all you need.
We will discuss this in detail later.

Day 60 -----> **1 + 2 +3 = You're Own Working Business**

To Review:

Q. What is Wealth Innovative?
A. A business model which entails any individual with no required experience to begin a local construction & remodeling company by simply finding a local builder who was overwhelmed by the current recession, and re-pleneshing that builder with what he lost: the items needed to operate his business.

Q. WHAT <u>EXACTLY</u> DO I NEED TO DO?
A. PROVIDE A LOCAL BUILDER WITH THE THREE ITEMS NEEDED TO OPERATE A BUSINESS.

THOSE ITEMS ARE:

1. Business License
2. Business Checking Account
3. Vendors (construction materials)

1. Business License

We've covered the required vendors in some great detail. Now, let's review how and why a GC needs a Business License. The Dwelling/General Contractors License is something that might not be necessary at all.

In addition to providing the GC with accounts at the required vendors, you might need to simply provide a business license for the GC to work under. Yes, this does mean that you have to get a GC License and Insurance. Do not get nervous. There are dozens of online classes and exams I recommend that are easier than you think. The GC license requires you take a course, which can be administered on the web.

Providing credit is 95% of the battle. However, often times a builder who has lost their credit likely accumulated personal liens or judgments. In most cases, a builder with a tax lien cannot reinstate their contractor's license.

Most states deny the registration of any certification, such as a contractor's license, if the applicant holds a tax lien. Call it a deterrent, punishment or just a way for the state to get paid. Even property tax liens take first priority when it comes to real estate practice. It doesn't matter if you have a $10 Million home, paid in cash, with no mortgage; if it has a property tax lien attached to it, you're not selling it. You won't be able to borrow $10 against it unless the local Municipality is paid.

Businesses or entities, like a contractor, whose net worth was depleted will have trouble paying debt. As explained earlier, these people folded on their mortgages as well as other payments, including taxes. Furthermore, small businesses try to deduct every expense possible to minimize steep taxes. The contractor is no different. However, the contractor was using every nickel to try to stay afloat, thinking this will pass. If it all passed, the contractor could just slash into his next set of profits to pay the state. However, the other side of the rainbow never came, the contractor spent all of the profits to keep his head above water, and the state never got paid. Talk about being kicked while you're down.

If a contractor owes state taxes, the state places a personal tax lien on his credit. The contractor wants to pay the state, but then he can't get licensed because of that very tax lien. How is the contractor supposed to pay the state if they keep him handcuffed? Talk about a catch-22. You can't call the governor and simply ask to be given a few months while you collect. That's just the way the system works. All just another reason why your local contractor needs your help.

Websites such as **www.contractor-licensing.com** lay everything out for you. All the pre-licensing materials can be printed, so you go through the motions, pass the online exam and print your certificate. This will vary by state. In some states, you are not required to take an exam. In others, you might not even need a certificate. If **www.contractor-licensing.com** cannot provide you with everything, simply check with your local 'Building Department'. It is not very hard to find out exactly what is needed. There is always a central location who administers licenses for all trades.

A General Contractors (or Dwelling Contractor) license simply allows a builder to pull permits. The true value of the Contractor's License lies in the building permit. In order to actually get a building permit, the construction must meet all codes. As opposed to a mason, for example, once you're licensed, your work isn't necessarily reviewed. It is for this reason that attaining a GC license is easier than you think. It only provides you with the *ability* to pull building permits. Whether or not your application is approved remains to be seen. However, that's not your concern! Your experienced builder is already familiar with the local code and how to construct a healthy project. However, without your license, he can't apply for a single thing. The won't even let your builder hang a picture if it means applying for a permit.

Getting a Driver's License is pretty easy to get, and so is a Contractor's License. However, there is one very big difference. With a Driver's License, after you pass, you don't have to take a test every time you want to drive a car. In order to use a Contractor's License, you must apply and be approved for a building permit. The building permit is, in a way, it's own test for every project. The beautiful part of Wealth Innovative is that you need not be concerned with getting building permits approved. Your job is to get a license so the builder is just in the position to apply for the building permits. We are not cutting corners or fooling the system. If getting around the building permit was part of the plan, we'd all be in big trouble. However, at the end of the day, all things are the same. The builder still has to get a building permit approved to move forward on any project.

The examinations for specific trades, such as HVAC or electrical are typically quite a bit more involved, and for good reason. It is those individuals who will actually be installing the plumbing, electrical, AC units, etc; not the builder! This may sound backwards to you, but it's not. The General Contractor needs to be familiar with local building code, safety, designs, etc. In many cases, a GC is not even on the actual site getting their own hands dirty. The general contractor is an overseer of all the installations and builds. If the GC doesn't know what he's doing, his designs will never be approved for a building permit. However, once they are approved, it is really up to the individual plumbers, electricians, excavators, concrete setters, HVAC Technician who hold themselves accountable for their own work. Sure, the builder is knowledgeable and could get by. However, every custom car shop will still have an individual brake, engine, tire, or paint guy.

Once you have passed the exam and print your credential, simply go to your state building or licensing institution and in 10 minutes….voila! They print your official license. If you don't think it's that easy, then why the heck did I even spend my time writing this whole thing? There is no reason why it should take 6 months to get a license. Outside of having to wait in line, you'll be all set.

The goal is to attain a license, not to learn how to build. If you want to learn how to build, feel free to attend about 2 years of trade school. After that, you'll need some real hard experience on job sites to slowly polish those skills. However, like me, I just wanted to OWN the business, which only requires a license.

This is the real miracle that you are offering your contractor. Many contractors lose their license because of tax liens and can no longer operate at all. I always looked at them as a Ferrari with no gas. They are full of potential and experience, just missing a little fuel. There is nothing wrong with employing a contractor with a tax lien.

Just because you have a license doesn't mean you can draw a house, let alone a dog-house. The people you employ (the GC, duh), are the real muscle in the operation, remember? Just let them do what they do best, Keep in mind, they operated for years without having some business partner tag alone like a sidecar. Every builder will be grateful, but if you're going to start asking them why they didn't go with the tan color siding instead of the white, your relationship will start growing fangs.

There are many contractors that lost their ability to work because of this failure. Many might work for another contractor or just be stuck in a rut. Like I said, a builder fought long and hard to earn their stripes. They have their own style. Don't be surprised to find builders who clash in opinion. This is why many might not work together. When they do it is like putting two dogs in a cage. There is nothing wrong with that. In fact, I can understand it. After all, there is a lot of art to building. Once the blueprints are created, there is a specific science. However, the blueprint is the list of ingredients.

The purpose of the GC license is NOT to determine if you know how to build a house or a cabinet. This is what people go to school. The actual license is to ensure that you follow safety and local building code. Most courses cover:

- Fire hazard

- Stairs and elevation hazards

- Building Code

- OSHA Requirements

That's it! It might sound like a lot or a little. However, it is all academic. The point is that passing the license is more of a formality, even for builders. It's almost like an athlete having to pass a physical. The true guts, the moneymaking engine is your GC business partner. Obviously, any business needs to comply with the state regulations

A GC license illustrates your understanding of local and state building code. Locating a builder is a topic we discuss in the next section. For now, let's simply discuss what you will need to do once you find the builder you'd like to reignite. The two of you will decide on a business name (ABC Builder, etc). In order to establish a business license you must acquire GC insurance.

GC License + GC Insurance = BUSINESS LICENSE.

The local 'Buildings Department' will tell you exactly what the minimum state insurance requirements are. Some states might require proof of a business checking account or other miscellaneous necessities. However, the most crucial are the GC license and GC Insurance. Your local insurance company will be able to help you. If you own a home or car, the insurance company who issued you a policy might be a great place to start. Ultimately, with that Business License you can employ whomever you like and the GC can pull permits with it.

This is the real kicker. Having that Business License in hand with your business partner is the tops. You are now a full-functioning building company.

The good news is that you can start pulling permits and jobs and let the good times roll. Jobs and profits will start rolling in. You'll need that business checking account for deposits.

The value of the Business License might exceed that of setting up vendors. 95% or more of projects will require a building permit. Any kind of addition, subtraction, overhang, garage installment, etc, will require the city's permission.

For example, you may remodel the interior of a kitchen. However any change to the structure of that kitchen will require a permit. Every home that is built requires city approval. The plans are inspected and they must satisfy the zoning. The particular zoning dictates the setback requirement, height, style, etc. You can't just build a 40 ft tall home that goes right up to the sidewalk. There could be a dozen different zonings all with different requirements. The zoning of a downtown will be different than that of a suburb subdivision. Also, if the home is next to a body of water, the project must conform to certain erosion dimensions. Water must flow away from a house at a specific angle and amount. Imagine a time when erecting a structure did not require proper zoning and inspection. Never mind the safety issues, one square block would look like a campground of tents, with each building sitting in a different position, one closer to the sidewalk than the other.

A building permit will always be issued to build that new home. It means the city is ok with the design. It could be 8 weeks later or 8 years later, but if you are making any kind of change to what the city initially approved, it must be checked once again. In addition to the planning and development approval or the site plan, the city also wants there additional money in property taxes.

The less pressing reason for a building permit is for a city to immediately re-assess the property. If you are adding 1,000 sq ft on finished space to the property, the city will be itching to tax that additional space. Avoid the building permit to save on property taxes and you're looking for some serious trouble. If the county gets wind of it, they'll shut you down. They might just go out of their way to be a pain in the ass with everything else you might want to do in the future. It's not worth it. Contrast to Table A, this is an illustration of how the company would operate with you as the credit provider:

2. Business Checking

It's best to keep your personal and business deposits completely separate. In order to open the business checking account, you will need a TIN (Tax Identification Number) and LLC. Both the TIN and LLC can be acquired online and in about 24 hours. The TIN is obtained through the IRS. Simply log onto the IRS website and navigate to the appropriate page.

Your local Department of Financial Institutions is responsible for issuing the LLC and LLC number. All these two items require you have a heartbeat and a credit card #. Expect to spend about $50. With the LLC, TIN and Driver's License you can open up the Business Checking Account. There is no specific account for general contractors. You are just another business opening up an account that is under the business name.

A Business Checking Account is necessary to cut checks to the subcontractors and vendors you will employ. That's pretty much it. Various banks offer business checking accounts with free monthly account analysis statements. The statements break down your spending, profit & loss, and other tools that could help manage your books.

3. Vendors

TABLE B

Subcontractor	Subcontractor	Subcontractor	Subcontractor	Subcontractor

Contractor

Licensed Business Owner

Roofing	Siding	Interior-design	Appliances	Dumpster	General-materials	Paint	Lumber/Milwork

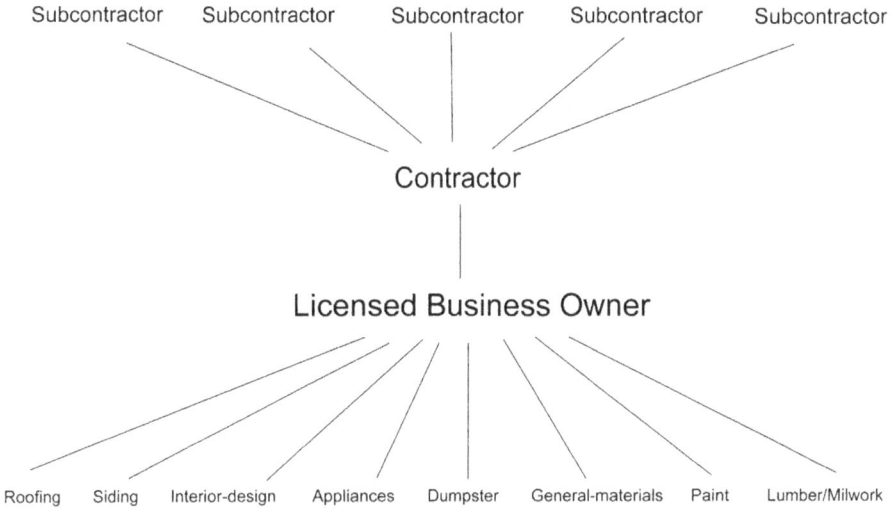

The most attractive characteristic of Wealth Innovative is that you are not to lending or putting up any significant real money because credit is used when there is a project!!

Building is a service industry! As explained earlier, the best part about a building company is the lack of necessary stock or moneys. Perhaps the builder has an account with funds to be used for advertising, general expenses. Otherwise, the builder is like a tailor, but for real estate. Bring the tailor a deal to renovate, and he only gets the materials needed for that job. No builder will stock lumber, kitchens, baths, etc. That is what the vendors are for!!

As you can see in Table B the only difference in the accounts setup is that they will be under your name with the builder as an authorized user of the accounts. Every credit account will have your address, with all bills sent to your home. This may seem overly simplistic, and to tell you the truth…it is! If a Builder doesn't have any credit, you do it for him.

Your first inclination might be hesitance to grant any authority to someone to use credit at a particular vendor. Ask yourself a few questions:

What the heck can the builder do with a credit account to a vendor like a paint store? Sell paint on the black market?

You just re-opened the flow of income for this GC. Why would he close it again?

You are not providing anybody with a line of credit! It would be one thing if you just handed someone checks and a credit card to an open line of credit. Then, they could misuse it. However, all you're doing is setting up credit accounts with specific places that sell specific items like tiles, windows, nails, and roof shingles!

This is not your typical business as you can tell. Moreover, you hold the checkbook at your disposal and all the bills are sent to your home. The vendors won't change any address on any account without your specific permission

To restate again, this opportunity was never really available before today. This particular recession is heavily real estate focused. The .com bubble burst, for example, had little to do with real estate.

How to Find YOUR Builder!

So you are ready to move forward, start your own real estate company and make a healthy return. That is fantastic! But wait, you need to find your business partner. The whole creative force of the company is missing. Don't be alarmed. The amounts of talented builders out there are abundant. The best part is you really only need one. JUST ONE. One talented, established GC to build a relationship with. This is not a team that you have to put together. One right fit and you'll never have to look back.

There are numerous ways to find your builder. Building or remodeling homes is what these builders do. Similar to a Doctor; once a builder, always a builder. Therefore, you don't have to worry that they have taken up cosmetology.

Perhaps you already know a builder. Maybe a friend of family member knows a builder. If not, below are the easiest places to start.

1. Realtor

Walk into any local real estate office and speak with a realtor. Ask the realtor to find a list of homes that are for sale that were unfinished new home builds. These new home builds were built by a builder who eventually couldn't finish them or went out of business. I guarantee you will have more than one to choose from. Moreover, have the realtor take you to those homes for a showing. This will allow you to see the build quality of all the different homes. Tell the realtor you're interested in working with a builder. Trust me, he or she will be very motivated to find one for you. The name of the builder will be readily available and I'm sure you can take it from there.

2. Bank

Local banks have lists of homes in foreclosure or short-sale, where a builder just couldn't finish or flip it. Speak with the mortgage banker or manager and ask for the REO properties (Real Estate Owned). When the builders fail, the houses don't just sit there! The banks will eventually acquire them with the hope of liquidating them. Sometimes they will employ the aforementioned local realtor to sell the home(s). In many cases, a realtor is not used and the home is only available through the bank. Either way, the bank is the #1 spot to find failed properties. Every single home, new or old, that foreclosed will eventually go back to the well. That well is the bank that lent the money for it. With that information, you'll discover who the builder was.

C. Subcontractors

Open the yellowpages and call some framing companies, roofers or plumbers. These guys do the work for contractors....existing and failed! They know of all the failed builders, big or small. In fact, these are the people who are most familiar with the local builders' work and reputation. The banks and realtors are trying to sell the homes. However, the subs personally know their builders.

When speaking with a sub , explain that you are a builder looking for some guys who went out of business. Moreover, ask for their suggestions. I wouldn't be surprised if these guys know builders who are looking for someone to work for....you! And guess what, these subcontractors might even have their phone numbers right in their cell phone. One visit to a job site might result in several contacts along with the subcontractor's suggestion as to whom they like to work for most.

You might visit a job site, start talking to a framer, and learn that he was actually a contractor that went out of business!!!! Like I said, builders are builders. They'll always be around building. Moreover, these guys need to make a living and pay the bills. If they can't build for themselves, many will just work under someone else's license for the paycheck. They might work as a simple tradesman just to get by.

D. Insurance Agents

With every contractor, comes an Insurance policy. You are looking for one builder out there. I truly believe it is easier done than said! Don't think or ruminate about it. He's the one in the tough position, not you!

C

How Wealth Innovative is Different from the Rest!!!

1. This is not 'Flip this House'

If you haven't realized by now that this isn't just another one of those real estate investment , 'get rich quick' gimmicks, this chapter will help. The #1 reason why this model is completely different is because just about every other book or guide relating to 'making money in real estate' is all about speculation.

'Flip this house', 'How to sell real estate', 'Making money in real estate', 'Buying and selling real estate', 'Flipping real estate', 'Flipping out on Real estate' or whatever attempt at a unique title; they are all just a number of keywords that you'll find online or in the bookstore. These models are identical because they entail investing your own money in the purchase of the real estate.

I throw caution to the wind when anyone mentions they are flipping property. All the shows on TV make it look so easy. From the comfort of your couch, you see some happy people come on the show and change a few things or completely remodel the home. The television show will supplement any drama with some dark background music. However, do you realize that these people ALWAYS sell it right away and they make money? Of course, it all occurs over the course of a one hour program with some silly commercials in between. Obviously it can't be done that quickly, but seeing it all happen in that one hour still creeps into your head. It must be so easy, right? WRONG! I hope by now you've realized that TV is so far from reality. It would be great if the show was two months long, they filmed the investors' sleepless nights, and it ends with the project simply not being finished. Now, that's reality.

What those shows don't show you is the strict budget that you must adhere to just to turn a profit. Or, how about the down payment and closing costs required just to attain ownership of the house in the first place. In most situations, the damn producers of the show pay for the remodeling, via advertisement money. They didn't show you the painstaking effort to find the right house, and really making sure they get the correct remodel to fit the budget of that neighborhood. It's BS!

Flipping homes is not easy and should be approached very carefully. If you don't get it right the first time, the budget is severely jeopardized and you lose money on the deal. Let's say you do finish the project. Now picture the anxiety of listing the house on the market and not getting any offers. You really do have to get it right the first time because experimenting isn't free. You can't change the bathroom, and then decide to knock it down and start over. Not only will it cost so much time, but the expenses will clean you out.

It takes tremendous experience and a good eye to be a successful house flipper. Not only do you need to really understand each neighborhood and subdivision, but be able to point out the good from the bad deal. Many houses will look the same, however the difference in opportunity is so different. Imagine two houses next to each other, for sale, that look alike, but one can turn profit and the other can turn you bankrupt. That is the reality.

Plenty of speculators made nice money in real estate. However, the market will never be the frenzy of 2004-2007; never! It was considerably easier to be in this business when homes were flying off the shelf. Investors would purchase a condo in Florida and make 150% in no time. Ask those same investors how the condos in Florida are doing. You'll find out the $250,000 condo is being liquidated for $110k.

Do yourself a favor and forget the past. It takes real brains and strategy to make money in real estate speculation these days. The secret is the eye of a builder who has the knowledge and experiences. Not only can he tell you what is feasible, but also the cost of what it could be done for. Don't wait for a working builder to be generous with this information either. Why would they share profitable information with an outsider? Would you? NOT UNLESS, YOU WERE THE BUSINESS PARTNER!!

The imprudent lending, which led to the boom, has dug us the biggest hole since the Great Depression. Not only is the market flooded with inventory, but it's also more expensive to flip homes. At one point you could borrow 95-100% of the purchase price, but those days are gone. Be prepared to put down a chunk of your savings. Are you prepared to throw $40k at a home, with one shot to get it right? You better know what you're doing. You are not Donald Trump with a load of inheritance money. Unlike you, he had the thickest safety net under him. Anybody with a safety net can write a book trivializing how easy it is to make money in real estate. Too bad they're so disconnected from the average person.

To reiterate, once again, the builder lost money because they built too many homes on speculation. Ask your builder how he will do things differently this time around and you'll grow more confident with each sentence. Sometimes the most progress is made by learning from one's mistakes. Unfortunately, the mistakes, in this case, were devastating.

Wealth Innovative is completely and utterly different. The risk is minimal and the cost is close to none. And best of all, eventually, you can get into the flipping game if you like. Let me clarify that last sentence: you and your talented, over-experienced builder of a business partner can eventually get into house flipping if you choose to. Wealth Innovative is the only real estate business model completely based on growing a business off a business partner. The business model of Wealth Innovative can apply to any industry. It just so happens that the model relates to real estate because it was real estate that was hit so hard in this unique way.

2. Credit is Renewable

We've established that the remodel business is built on credit. It's also common sense that money doesn't grow on trees. The expression 'money doesn't grow on trees' means that unlike leaves, which are renewable, money used never comes back. The leaves fall, grow back, fall and grow back over and over.

Credit, on the other hand, is renewable. If the business is built on credit, and credit is renewable, what does that mean? It means that you can do this more than once, folks. Contrarily, when opening a McDonalds or another franchise, you're putting all your eggs in one basket because the upfront cost is not renewable.

Multiplying the business by doing the same thing with multiple contractors is easy. Can you even imagine the benefits of co-owing 3 businesses? Not only are you spreading the already minimal risk, but you're more versatile. Perhaps one contractor specializes in X, with another better at Z. The potential is nearly endless.

Earlier, I asked you to imagine owning a piece of a contracting company that was flourishing 3 years ago. That level of action could be right back on it's feet in no time, with ownership at the bottom floor of that company for the next 10+ years. Now, picture being in that position with 2, 3 or 4 companies. It's not impossible at all.

The opportunities are endless. Perhaps you and the builder would like to venture into another source of income. When things are going well, doors will start opening up for you. Maybe you'll eventually want to purchase a franchise or try your hand at a new business. Having the foundation of income from your contracting business will allow you to make those decisions. The financial security that your contracting business provides will allow you to venture into riskier businesses. Perhaps there is a company you'd like to start up with a friend or colleague. Maybe you'd like to buy land in a location where you believe will eventually be very desirable. The possibilities are endless.

I cannot explore all the hypothetical possibilities. I'll leave that up to you. And perchance, one day, it'll be your turn to start something unique and write all about it!

3. Greater Potential

First of all, just about all of the aforementioned real estate books were written during the boom times. So if you haven't thrown them out already, please do so now. They are antiquated.

Real Estate demands its due respect. It is not something that just remains the same in any market. Unlike gold, silver or any other commodity, real estate is fluid. The demand changes, the styles and current fashions always change. Take a drive through older neighborhoods and even 10-15 year old homes stand out.

The knowledge and experience required to grow on your own takes quite some time. Perhaps the biggest issue with 'real estate flip' books is its limitations. These guides attempt to illustrate how to buy and sell some real estate. However, that's where it ends. In the case you are successful at flipping real estate, what are you supposed to do then?

When working with a talented and experienced contractor, you will learn the DNA of real estate. Moreover, once you've moved through a few real estate speculations, your appetite might grow. Perhaps some multi-units might be of interest. How about a development? Yes, a development such as a row of businesses with rentals above is not difficult once you're familiar with how basic principles such as land division utilities, and zoning work.

Every new aspect of real estate will be a little challenging. However, you adapt and move onto something more complicated. For some reason, babies want to learn how to walk and run. It's an innate characteristic. You will eventually look at real estate speculation and laugh. Those real estate 'flip' books will be a joke to you.

Building a house demands specific people like plumbers, roofers, excavators, electricians, HVAC, etc. Development is the same thing, however, on a larger scale. A team of people works on a development. However, if your experience in real estate doesn't start with a healthy foundation, you'll never get there.

A portfolio of remodels, spec homes, developments, or multi-units will turn you into a robust investor. Simply focusing on flips is elementary. It's static and unfertile. You'll never grow. You will develop along with your business and with your experienced contractor!

Q and A's

1. How can I really be sure we won't fold?

To reiterate, builders did not lose their credit from the accounts they had set up. They lost their credit from borrowing too much money from the banks to build too many homes on speculation! The builders lost their credit, and eventually lost all their accounts. They were then sitting ducks.

Remodeling homes is 100% based on using the client's money. It is not like selling cars where a dealer will have to buy 20 cars and pray that he can sell them. You are not putting money up-front. In fact, it is more of a 100% custom-car shop, however without having to stock rims, tires, and paint. To take it a step further, you actually use the client's garage and all his tools to do customize the car! This business is like no other. All the work involves **their** home. And all the work is done at **their** house. How much simpler can it be? A remodel or newly built home is the safest way to earn a commission. The client pays the GC for everything.

Speculation is the only way to risk credit. Spec homes are more similar to the car dealer purchasing 20 cars in the hope the buyers come along. The issue rises when you are leveraging, 3,4, 5+ homes. Even worse is when those homes are your very luxury, upscale, $500k+ deals. You can build $150k spec homes and likely sell them. The idea of buying a newly completed built home is a great sale. Why buy a 15 year old house, even a 3 year old house when you can get brand new?

2. What kind of profit split between my business partner and I do you suggest?

This is a case by case situation. You can offer different splits depending on the amount of work each of you contribute. The whole point is that the GC is using your license and your credit. Some might suggest a 75/25 split, 70/30. or 50/50.

Don't get too mixed up with the split. The GC you are working with is doing all or most of the work. You are getting paid for providing the tools necessary. It is not worth getting greedy. You can be on an island in the Bahamas for 6 months earning your split, while your GC is working his tail off. The split needs to be in his or her favor because he or she is really taking on the entire burden. Be grateful that you are on the bottom floor of a business in the first place. 5 years later, your minimal percentage split could be 20 times more than what you're making putting 100% time into your job at ABC Make Money For Somebody Else Company

If you are familiar with the building trade, or have learned it, that is a completely different dynamic. Working on-site, or being a project manager can earn you a larger split. Keep in mind, bringing in the business needs to be rewarded. A good builder will be the one that sells the client on his design and his price. When your builder is pulling in $30k a month in commission, which you get to split, be appreciative.

3. Who controls the checkbook and accounting?

You do. It's your business and it's your business account. Every subcontractor issues a bid for any job. That bid is essentially an invoice. Once their work is completed, you will pay the subcontractor and receive a receipt of payment.

It is really best to make sure the books are clean and organized. Real Estate is not incredibly complex, however, better account management may have helped a builder or two foresee that he was slowly losing profits.

The profit of a transaction is a delicate balance of costs. With one mistake, you can overshoot the budget and then start digging into your own pocket. Some builders just shoot from the hip and order things on the fly which is just a disaster waiting to happen. Not only can you start losing profit, but spend too much, and you'll be paying the owner to do the job!

When purchasing a franchise, the workflow or accounting might be set up for you as part of the $1 Million you had to for over. This is more of a 'learn as you go' scenario. Get yourself a good bookkeeper if balancing the books is too much to handle.

4. How do I know what vendors are needed?

Your builder will know exactly what is needed for every single job and where to get it from. Typically, you'll have more than one choice for any account needed. Having several lumber accounts established is not a bad idea either.

Remember, you're not spending anything unless it's ordered for a pre-determined project. A builder can literally operate an entire business not owning more than a few tools!! Every other darn thing is ordered only per what the specific job requires. And every single piece of material is paid for using the client's money!!

This is a turn-key operation because the builder has already been in operation for 5, 15+ years. If you were to buy a Franchise, all the vendors are supplied to you. For example, a Walgreens or a McDonalds all function the same way. The same exact way. When investors purchase their own franchise, everything is handed down to them like manuals to a new car. Same thing applies here. You'll be all set-up, using your builder's knowledge and experience on your side.

6. Do we need an Office?

No. You do not need an office. In the future, it is certainly convenient to have an office where documents, plans, or meetings can all take place. However, almost all subs and builders do not have an office. For now, it is best to be on the frugal side with your expenses.

The beautiful aspect of this business is that ALL the work is done at the client's home. If anything is fixed, it is done at the client's home. All the initial meetings to plan, design, sell the client on your drawing…... is all done at the client's home. You could literally live in your truck and still present yourself as a competent company. I wouldn't suggest it, but the point is that this is not your typical business!

The upfront costs of a contracting company is minimal. The builder has worked many years to develop his routine and it typically involves utilizing an office. You can always look for a cheap rental office in the future. But unlike starting a restaurant, shoe store, Dr's office, clothing store, mechanic, health club, grocery store, or salon, you don't need an office.

What about the furnaces, air conditioners, cabinets, appliances, extra; don't you need to store that somewhere? NO!!! You order the lumber from the lumberyard two days before framing. The HVAC subcontractor provides all the furnaces, a/c, extra. Your local appliance dealer (like a Best Buy) will deliver the appliances (with their truck!) the day you request them.

I've compared this project to a Franchise because they are both turn-key models. Of course, there are a few significant differences. Examples of Franchises are purchasing a:

- McDonalds

- Wendy's

- Anytime Fitness

- Gold's Gym

Call the corporate office, plunk down a chunk of change and you can have your own business. It's a solid investment and sure to prosper. You are just pulling a slice off an already established name that is proven. The risk is minimal.

You purchase a Franchise, turn the key, open the doors and you can expect business. Hence, it is a turn-key business. If you start your own restaurant with your own name, you have to start from the very bottom and work your way up. You'll have to earn the reputation and service that a major franchise already has. You'll have to start where McDonalds and Wendy's did 75 years ago. The challenge is tremendous.

Owning a contracting company with an established builder is your Turn-key business. However, there is a substantial difference. The upfront expenses of a contracting company are negligible. You do not have to provide $1mm to purchase the business. You certainly do not have to open a location with expensive rent and hire staff. This is why the contracting company is such a unique opportunity. What's the best part of the deal? You put more profit into your pocket.

When owning a franchise, it is a constant balancing of the monthly expenses. The projects come in, you then source out the staff. This is completely vice-versa with a franchise where you have to hire the staff first and then bring in the business to offset the costs.

The contracting company is almost a fantasy operation. Where can you book the work first, and then hire the labor?? I'd like to see the owner of a McDonald's wait for an order of a Big Mac and then hire staff to make it! The contracting company is perhaps the most efficient system available. Anybody can do it. Moreover, you don't have to spend your day at the McDonald's to ensure everything is working well. You can keep your full-time job, sit back and do what your like. It is really up to you.

There is virtually nothing to manage with this system. When business does come in, your business partner (GC) is the manager on-site overseeing everything. I explained this earlier when I laid out a project from A to Z. Here, we are revisiting the idea of a build being similar to a small operating company, with the GC serving as the manager of the process. The efficiency is the true hallmark of this Turn-key business.

7. <u>Can the builder use profits to pay off his own vendor accounts to get them in good standing?</u>

The reason you are afforded this fantastic opportunity is because a builder folded due to overleveraging his business. However, all the money and profit from a job is paid to you. Remember, this is your company, not the builders. It's your name on the LLC, TIN, business checking account, and all the vendors. His name is no where to be found because he simply works for you.

If an employee of your local grocery store racked up debt, would the owner of the grocery store have to pay his employee's debts? Obviously not! It's exactly the same thing here. Exactly the same! The builder is the creative force, but he owns nothing.

On another note, the good news is that there is certainly more than one vendor in town for the various applications. I'm sure you'll find more than one lumber, carpet or paint shop.

8. What else besides credit might you need to establish an account with the various vendors?

You'll find that certain vendors will request several references. Most likely, they will follow through with checking on that reference. Therefore, ask your builder for 2-3 subcontractors that he uses on a regular basis and is in good standing with. He instructs those subcontractors that XYZ vendor might call.

The only other request a vendor might make is for your bank account information and authorization to check the status. The vendor would like to see that you have not been delinquent for the majority of the time. As a last resort, if things fall apart, they'd feel comfortable knowing you have a few bucks in your account to help pay down the balances.

9. How are monies dispersed, i.e., profit earned?

Profit will be earned in the form of a General Contractor Fee. The GC Fee can range from 10-25%, depending on the type of work being done. A standard, relatively simple project might return a profit of 10%. If you are building a new home for a client, you will likely not be able to charge more than 12%.

The larger the job, the more your GC fee will be scrutinized. A buyer paying $350,000 to build his home will likely be counting his pennies more than the client just finishing his basement. It's really a case-by-case situation which your builder will be most familiar with.

In any event, the GC fee is the profit. This is essentially the only income stream you really have to be concerned with. Unless the contractor will be working on-site, paying himself on an hourly basis, there will not be another form of payment. A Dentist, Doctor, tailor, etc, has one fee…..their service fee.

When a project begins, you will likely not see an income deposit for a few weeks when the first draw is taken out. Sometimes everything is paid upfront, which is a different situation. When someone is using a bank loan to fund the remodel, all money is dispersed through an escrow account.

The job begins and work is done. After a few weeks or so, it is time to reimburse the subs, labor, materials etc, for what was done. A draw request is then sent to the escrow or title company. That company will hire an inspection service to drive over to the site to check to make sure that the work you are claiming was actually performed. After all, they are protecting the interests of the bank, who do not want to just lend money for any work not done yet. The inspection service will check off that the work is done, money is dispersed, and you pick up your check.

Sometimes the GC fee is collected at the end of the job. Or, you can have the GC fee dispersed throughout the project as installments within each draw. Therefore, you can earn a 'paycheck', being the owner of the company, every few weeks as if it were a real job. Once you start putting together several projects you'll be wagging your tail in excitement.

The income that can be produced is extraordinary. The basic contractor can earn $125,000 simply because of the materials he has. A contractor with experience and some talent can bring in upwards of $350k. It really depends on how aggressive you and the builder are. IF you really go after it, you can really do some damage!

10. There is likely a stigma working with someone who obviously failed. How do we get off on the right foot?

There are some questions that I am always asked. Such as 'Didn't, he lose everything? Is he in jail? What ever happened to X, Y or Z? I later became immune to the negative impressions.

I recently went to a local bar on a Saturday night just for a few beers to mellow out, and watch the football game. The bartender, Joe, and I started to just shoot the breeze as they say. One conversation and topic leads to another and I mention my career path, etc. Would you know it, the Joe is in the building trade. I explain that I'm doing business with Dave where I immediately get cut off with "Dave?! You're doing business with him?!". I proudly admit that I am working with Dave and things are going well.

The bartender happens to be a past sub of Dave. They worked many jobs together before everything tumbled. Joe is so curious, asking me question after another. The whole time, I'm wondering to myself, 'aren't you supposed to listen to my day?'. In any event, Joe proceeds to reminisce about the day when things were flowing like water.

Joe had moved on with his own contracting company. Apparently, rumor had it that Dave was not doing well, to say it kindly. Mind you, I'm hearing all this gossip from the guy serving me drinks at the local dive. With conviction, I tell him exactly what the past year has been like. The events of the last 2 years are so unique and convoluted that we might never make sense of it.

Joe tried to explain how bartending created opportunities for him to recruit contracting business. My response to the guy who questioned my partner's reputation was not kind, to say the least. After 30 minutes Joe was handing me his business card asking to connect me with Dave. He pretty much followed me out the door dictating his resume to me.

The point is that the vast majority of people are afraid and ill-informed. Your association with an individual who went bankrupt might scare others. It's amazing how people maxed out on credit cards, getting absolutely nowhere, walking the same darn tight rope for years, will judge someone who was living it up and went for it all. They quickly forget the circumstances of the market, the 16% unemployment rate in Detroit, the millions of people who lost their job.

Walking the straightest line might produce less risk for potential failure or exposure. There is nothing wrong with that decision. It's safe, convenient and completely predictable. Many people don't even have that opportunity in itself.

Confidence is incredibly contagious. According to Forbes, almost two-thirds of the world's 946 billionaires made their fortunes from scratch, relying on grit and determination, and not good genes. Directly from Forbes: Fifty self-made tycoons are college or high school dropouts. The most famous billionaire dropout is Microsoft's Bill Gates, who finally got his honorary degree from Harvard University in June, 30 years after quitting the prestigious school to sell software. "I did the best of everyone who failed," joked the world's richest man in his official graduation address. With failure like that, who needs success?

Ask every millionaire if they ever took a big loss. I'll guarantee almost all of them did. I'd make that bet because the only way you can become so successful is by taking risk. No risk equals no reward; we've all heard it. And with Wealth Innovative being one of the most minimal risking taking ventures, I personally plan on doing this 10 times more!

11. <u>Why wouldn't a builder just work under an already established contractor's license?</u>

> There are likely a number of builders that had no choice but to consolidate their efforts by working under another contractor. In fact, that was probably their only choice up to that point. The issue is that they have settled for an hourly wage or commission that is diluted compared to what they were earning on their own.

> Rarely will an established contractor split their profits with an unlicensed builder who just lost it all. Call it what you will, but the builder is now an employee of that primary contractor. The same thing might occur between real estate brokers. In some cases, a broker can no longer keep his doors open, so he works under another brokers' license. It's called an associate broker relationship.

> Unlike you or I, the primary contractor has had an established business for quite some time. It is too late for that failed builder to get in at the bottom level of the company. You can bet that the primary contractor won't split his profits with the associate contractor. When you come along and offer the contractor half a loaf, he'll pounce on it.

> Later I will explain the role of sub-teams, which is a slow accumulation of labor to help with the increasing client demands. The failed builder working for another contractor will essentially be treated to the same compensation as those sub-teams. That's not what they want, but don't have a choice.

12. <u>Can't the builder go to the bank for startup capital?</u>

> No! Even 3 years ago, banks would not grant startup capital to an individual who just failed or has poor credit. The risk of capital is unlike a real estate or even a car loan because it's unsecured. Unless the builder was putting up something of real value for collateral, he doesn't stand a chance.

> Most importantly, the business is based on very basic credit, not startup capital. The capital used is from the homeowner or soon to be homeowner. Therefore, the credit is really the assembly line of the business, but the builder lost it.

> What's even better is that credit is much more accessible than any startup capital. Startup capital is exceptionally more risky than just offering credit. Also, it could take months to even gain access to startup capital, whereby credit is literally available with a stroke of a pen

CHAPTER VII

Grow your Business

When you and your experienced builder establish the name of the company and set up all the necessary vendors you'll be so excited to get going. In my opinion, the hard part is over. Many people would be envious to be in this position. Of course, it is really worthless unless the business starts pouring in. Luckily, it is not very difficult.

Many homeowners are looking to remodel their home or build new. The media will report how home sales are down, mortgage lending is down, everything is down. From the comfort of your couch, you can be convinced that everything is going down the tubes. You almost don't want to leave the house the way they make you feel!

Here is some food for thought: Compared to how many loans were written and homes were sold during the boom, of course it's going to be down!! It'll never be that active again for heaven's sake. That's what got us into trouble in the first place, and now we are complaining about it. Trust me, there are tons of remodels and home sales occurring every day. In fact, it will get even busier as time goes on.

Mortgage lending is definitely harder to come by. It will eventually loosen, but for the time being it is certainly tighter. Now, the word 'tighter' shouldn't be confused with the word 'doomed'. It's tighter than it was in 2003-2007. However, millions of dollars are still lent on a daily basis. Yes, banks are still lending amounts of money that would make you salivate.

Another huge by-product of the current market is the abundance of home sellers. As opposed to having multiple buyers fighting over one property, you'll now have multiple sellers fighting over one buyer. What does this mean for your business? This is fantastic news for the remodelling industry. In fact, it is the super-boom times for remodel. Why? Because sellers need to do whatever they can to distinguish their home from the next one down the street. Sellers used to offer cars, vacations, whatever they could to sell a home. However, who the heck wants a car that they'll have to pay taxes and spend gas on? Who wants a vacation that they don't have time to enjoy? **I'll tell you what the buyer wants: a nicer home!**

Finishing basements, remodeling kitchens, or installing 4-season porches are just the basic types of remodels that home sellers may opt for.

The remodeling and new construction business is out there for the taking. Most of all, there are less builders and contractors fighting for that business. If you still think recessions are bad, consider why you're in this position in the first place. Without a recession, every contractor would either never return your call, or they'd tell you to take a hike. However, now, they need your help. Moreover, the recession washed away the phonies. Your builder had plenty of business before and likely knows exactly where to get more. When people find out that he is back in business, you'll likely be busier than you anticipated. A builder who is back on his feet is a sign of tremendous strength. People will look at him as if he was meant to be.

Remember, it wasn't the lack of business that killed the builder. He took on too many properties and buyers couldn't qualify for those loans anymore. People still want to buy or build a new home. Instead of building 5-10 homes and waiting for the buyers to come, the contractor understands the value of pacing themselves.

I would highly suggest putting together a website that really highlights your business and the services that your provide. Today's media is heavily internet-based, with the newspaper going out of style. Check out www.godaddy.com and use some of their templates. With your builders help, you could put together something pretty simple , but effective.

With all the current and future homeowners waiting to hire your business, several approaches can be taken to reel them in:

1. Advertising

Simple postcard advertising from an online company is a no-brainer. You can literally paint a whole subdivision at a time with postcards advertising one specific type of remodel. The postcard should direct the consumer to the website where they can find more material, including the company contact information.

Home Building magazines are another option. Some remodel businesses have thrived very well just advertising with this type of media. These magazines will target clients within a specific range of home value and total household income. Like I said, they are very effective and often times all that is necessary to launch the business for a company.

2. Realtors

There might be one person who actually would love to sell the home more than the actual client: the Real Estate Agent. No sale results in no commission to the Realtor.

Sale results in commission. It's as simple as that. Second to the IRS First Time Home Buyer Tax Credit, a remodel might be the agent's best friend. Advertising to the real estate agents is a sure fire way to get business your way.

If you can help a realtor sell one home, they will be ringing your phone to get you the next deal or two. Therefore, establishing relationships with the local realtors could result in repeat business for years to come. After all, they are working in the same field as you are. Offer realtors and brokers free walk throughs and estimates. An advertisement might not work for many people because each individual house is unique and you're expecting the homeowner to self-diagnose what their house is missing. Actually getting in there and showing the seller, on paper, what remodel is needed will really make a difference getting them fired up.

3. Building Credit

After you open the business checking account, you'll be depositing money pretty often. With these deposits, you'll be building business credit with the bank. When applying for a personal loan, the bank will use your FICO score to determine credibility. Your income is obviously important, but banks will analyze how you've paid back debt in the past.

Business credit is quite different in comparison to personal credit.. In the future, you'll want to borrow against the business. After you've established the income history, you'll be able to demonstrate how the money will be paid back. In contrast to a business loan, a personal loan can be affected by your other debts. A business lender will know that creditors of your personal debt cannot influence or go after the business debt.

Why would you want to borrow against the business? Well, perhaps you'll want to build a spec home in the future. A speculation home can result in a very nice profit for your company.

I've established the danger in building too many speculation homes. However, building and selling one at a time can provide lucrative business. I would never recommend real estate speculation to anybody new to real estate. However, your builder of a business partner makes your company worthy and prepared to take the next step. Taking on risk is not for everybody. Over time, and after years of doing well and appreciating your builder's talent, perhaps you'll feel comfortable taking that step. Remember, it's all up to you.

4. Become a Realtor

You might ask yourself, 'I have a building company, why would I waste my time getting a realtors license?' The two are so interlinked and can offer a huge leg up. Having a realtors license in itself is useful. You can list a home or represent a buyer at your own pace and make a few bucks. In addition, it keeps you tied into the local real estate market.

We discussed building a spec home after you've developed some business credit. Well, who do you think is the best person to list that home? You!! Not only can you sell it, but you can find the land or home to remodel on your own. Why give 3-6% away when you can just do it yourself?

A real plus is being able to offer your clients remodelling advice and service. Few realtors are tied into a building company. If you like, you can offer to list clients' homes at a discount rate if they remodel their home with your company. It certainly makes sense to the client because they are killing two birds with one stone. They are also saving a big chunk of change!

Lastly, having a realtors license gives you access to the local Multiple Listing Service (MLS). The MLS is such a powerful tool to have when owning a building company. If you learn more about the MLS, you'll realize how much information can be obtained in your local market.

The most apparent use of the MLS would be to pull searched of dated home listings. Homes listed for say, 120+ days, will make sellers begin to itch. Target those people for a remodel. As 120 turns into 180 days, trust me, they'll be calling you. You can potentially work on getting the listing or help them buy their next home (or build a new home!). The MLS will allow you to print labels, search by subdivision, etc. Simply having the license is a real asset.

I mentioned earlier how growing realtor contacts is a true asset. There is no way easier than being a realtor yourself. Again, it could be a 5 hour a week position, but at least you're plugged into the scene. The word will get out quickly.

Sub-Teams

The worst case scenario will be generating so much business that you and the builder are overwhelmed. What a nightmare, huh?! This is really when the company can turn into a living, breathing machine. A machine that can consistently grow without you. Something an individual Franchise can only dream of.

When your business starts to do well your builder will be plenty busy. With the added influx of business from further advertising, you'll really be swamped. The last position you want to be in is not being able to handle the volume. You will generate a poor reputation and you might start dropping the ball on the business you've already established. This business is supposed to make your life easier, not harder.

I mentioned the subs that are contracted carry out most of the labor. If you are in the position where business is routine, you can offer to hire these subs directly under you. Up until now, these subs had their own operation and they sent you a bill for their labor. A problem with this system is that they are sub-contracted out; which means you are not the only business hiring them for work. There are likely other contractors in town booking them for work as well. It's imprudent to feel slighted when a subcontractor has to leave your site for a competitor's. However, that's how it works. You can't expect the subs to put all their eggs in one basket.

This is where building sub-teams could be a viable option. Actually hiring these people will give you 100% control over the labor. You won't have to worry about coordinating schedules with materials and clients getting a little restless. The sub-team could be the same 4-5 guys that always work together.

In addition to having the sub-team you can have one time entirely devoted to a specific type of remodel. Perhaps one team only does basement finishing. I'm sure you can imagine the added benefit. Besides building an incredible rapport, the team will become exceptionally efficient at what they do. They'll manage multiple jobs at a faster rate. It'll make the job better, a happier client, and earn your company the best reputation in town.

Designers:

The most important element is getting the client signed on the dotted line. Your builder has experience drawing, planning out designs. Subs are just not made to draw or design. They show up on an already prepared job site, with all systems go. You give them the tools, a blueprint, wind the string on their back and let them loose.

Your local trade school is one place you can tap for those drawing skills. Plenty of students are enrolled in drafting and drawing classes. You'll want a student that has some experience in the field and doesn't just know how to sit in front of a desk. Some real exposure really helps round out the feasibility and sell of their design. Either way, these academically trained individuals are a pretty good way to bring in some affordable talent.

CHAPTER VIII

Snowball

Word will spread very quickly, especially when you are doing well. Advertising or earning realtor contacts will get people through the proverbial door. However, I guarantee that the business will snowball. One job will turn into two. Two can turn into 5. When people see your lawn signs and the quality of work, 5 can turn into 15.

Recall that there are fewer contractors out there. When your name becomes a commonality around town, people will want to contract your company. It's human nature to want to be a part of something that everybody else has. And, for very good reason. If other builers are doing it, you must be offering superior designs.

The builder has been there before. And most likely, he or she will be able to get right back to that level of action pretty quickly. He is probably itching to get real busy but just hasn't figured out how to get the doors open again. If he got to a certain point before, you can guarantee he or she wants to get there again.

I immediately noticed the plethora of contacts that my builder had attained over the course of his career. It was very impressive. People found out that he was back in action and it was all we needed. People are often impressed that the builder is back on his feet. It's a serious sign that he's meant to be in this business. Like I said, everything was running full steam before I got there. All I did was fire it back up and step back!

The first chapters encompassed the idea of planting the seed immediately so it can grow like wildfire later. If you get the seed planted now, you will eventually have a bigger piece of the pie. It's much easier negotiating a seed than when it is a full-grown tree. There is room for some experimentation now. It's like learning how to drive late at night vs. rush hour. It's still quiet with the current state of market. However, when it all turns around, you can bet it will be much harder to maneuver around.

Do not be hesitant. Take advantage of this opportunity because it won't last long. We've injected $800mm into this country's economy and there might be more. Never mind how long it will take to pay it off, if we ever do. The point is that everybody wants to return to glory; me, you, the public, the politicians, and the rest of the globe. Remember, with a capitalist country, things can really only go one way; up or down. It got bad, but it will get better. It has to. If we don't get the water out of the boat, it will sink. Rest assured, we'll all be back on our feet, but that is when things get trickier.

This is a truly a chance of a lifetime. Take what you want now.

Eventually, the sellers market will turn into a buyers market. Everything will be the opposite. Here's a well known tip: when everybody is selling, BUY. When everyone is buying, SELL. It applies to everything including stocks and real estate.

You'll be kicking yourself when all of a sudden you have to wait in line again for your opportunity. The rich will be getting richer when this is all over. Don't wait ten years for the next opportunity. Do it now.

Good luck!

Appendix I

Consult with your contractor for a list of vendors at the local level. The LLC is filed at the State level, typically with the Department of Financial Regulations. A quick search on your web browser will send you in the right direction.

The EIN (or TIN) as well as the LLC can all be filed online. In fact, the following resources will help you get just about everything necessary to get the company set up.

Website Development..www.Godaddy.com

Business Postcards.. www.Postcardmania.com

Contractor License.. www.Contractor-Licensing.com

TIN.............................. http://www.irs.gov/businesses/small/article/0,,id=97860,00.html

Contracts ....www.legalzoom.com

Contractor Agreements ....www.lawdepot.com

You may visit one of Josh Bieber's companies,

all based on the Wealth Innovative model, at:

www.24-7DesignBuild.com

(Please do not submit any comments on the website, or call the office phone number.

This is strictly reserved for the company's local clients)

Thank You!